GENERATION BLEND

GENERATION BLEND

Managing Across the Technology Age Gap

ROB SALKOWITZ

WILEY

John Wiley & Sons, Inc.

For general information on our other products and services, or technical support, please contact our Customer Care Department within the United States at 800-762-2974, outside the United States at 317-572-3993 or fax 317-572-4002.

Wiley also publishes its books in a variety of electronic formats. Some content that appears in print may not be available in electronic books.

For more information about Wiley products, visit our Web site at http://www.wiley.com.

Library of Congress Cataloging-in-Publication Data:

Salkowitz, Rob 1967-
   Generation blend : managing across the technology age gap / Rob Salkowitz.
      p.   cm.
   Includes index.
   ISBN 978-0-470-19396-9 (cloth)
   1. Older-people–Employment. 2. Older-people–Attitudes. 3. Technological innovations. 4. Technology and older people. 5. Management. I. Title,
   HD6279.S25 2008
   658.30084–dc22

                                                                    2007045582

Printed in the United States of America

10   9   8   7   6   5   4   3   2   1

To my parents . . . from one generation to another.

Microsoft Executive Leadership Series: Series Foreword

The Microsoft Executive Leadership Series provides leaders with inspiration and examples to consider when forming business strategies to stand the test of time. As the pace of change quickens and the influence of social demographics, the impact of educational reform, and the impetus of national interests evolve, organizations that understand and embrace these underlying forces can build strategy on solid ground. Increasingly, information technology is bridging social, educational and international distances, and empowering people to perform at their fullest potential. Organizations that succeed in the enlightened use of technology will increasingly differentiate themselves in the marketplace for talent, raw materials, and customers.

I talk nearly every day to executives and policy makers grappling with issues like globalization, workforce evolution, and the impact of technology on people and processes. The idea for this series came from those conversations-we see it as a way to distill what we've learned as a company into actionable intelligence. The authors bring *independent* perspectives, expertise, and experience. We hope their insights will spark dialogues within organizations, among communities, and between partners about the critical relationship between people and technology in the workplace of the future.

I hope you enjoy this title in the Microsoft Executive Leadership Series and find it useful as you plan for the expected and unexpected developments ahead for your organization. It's our privilege and our commitment to be part of that conversation.

Daniel W. Rasmus

General Editor, Microsoft Executive Leadership Series

Contents

Preface

The seed of this book was first planted toward the end of 2003. At that time, I was working as a business writer and communication consultant on projects for a variety of high-tech and software companies. Dan Rasmus, an analyst for Giga Research, whom I had encountered in some of my work, had just been hired at Microsoft in the intriguing position of Director of Information Work Vision. I contacted him and shortly found myself involved in an ambitious project to chart out the social, political, and economic implications of information technology over the next 10 to 15 years. Demographic trends, particularly the uncertainties generated by the arrival of the Millennials in the workforce, were a major focus of our research.

Around the same time, I received a call from my old friend Tom Kamber. Tom was working as executive director for a nonprofit that provided technology assistance for low-income people in New York City, but he was growing dissatisfied with both the organization and its approach. A recent experience had convinced him that the digital *age* gap was even more pronounced than the economic digital divide, but no organization in New York was set up specifically to address the needs of older adults. He said he was looking into forming his own organization called Older Adults Technology Services (OATS) to spread technology skills, awareness, and workforce development assistance to people over age 50 who felt disconnected from the high-tech world. When he invited me to join the Board of Directors, I leapt at the chance.

Over the next few years, I delved deeper into the issues of age and technology from these two different perspectives. My work with Dan exposed me to the whole range of generational scholarship and theory, including the groundbreaking analysis of William Strauss and Neil Howe, and Don Tapscott's Seminal work on the Net Generation, as well as the methodologies of scenario planning popularized by the Global Business Network. OATS familiarized me with the practical, human side of the equation: the day-to-day experiences of older workers and the successful methods for getting them past their fears and frustrations through specific training approaches and intergenerational dialogue.

When Microsoft solicited proposals for a book series on people and technology, the concept of *Generation Blend* seemed like a natural one. There was plenty of material about generational factors in the workplace and lots of books written on new Web 2.0 technologies, but nothing I could find connected these two significant trends. My personal connections with OATS and the group within Microsoft that ran the Board of the Future project gave me two unique sources of primary data. It was the perfect marriage of means, motive, and opportunity. Since I am not a sociologist or IT professional, and have limited first-hand experience with management, I spent a lot of time reviewing the literature and researching the many facets of this vast subject. I also interviewed as many experts, analysts, experienced professionals, and technology users of various ages as I could find. My hope is to focus this range of data and opinion into a coherent presentation for organizational decision-makers facing the challenges of managing across the digital age gap in a fast-changing world.

I'm certainly grateful to Microsoft for nominating me to write this title in the series. Microsoft's philosophy of putting people at the center of technology represents a genuinely affirmative approach in a world where business often appears eager to reduce people to the role of interchangeable parts and low-cost commodities. But the goal of this book is not to sell the benefits of Microsoft software or the virtues of Microsoft as a company. You will find in these pages nary a mention of Microsoft technology, or that of any other vendor.

This is not a book about IT. It's a book about people, generations, and the transformative impact of new ways of communicating, collaborating, and managing information. Whether the technology emanates from Microsoft, Oracle, Google, or an Open Source community, its impact on people, organizations, and societies poses the same potential challenges and opportunities.

I hope that *Generation Blend* provides some useful perspectives for organizational leaders who are grappling with these issues. At the very least, it was my honor and privilege to give voice to the various people of all ages who contributed their insights and their time, because in the end, those authentic voices remind us that the technology exists to serve *us* and *our* needs. When we forget that in the rush for economic advantage, we have forgotten something very important about being human.

Rob Salkowitz
Seattle, WA
February 2008

1

Introduction

The themes of age and technology are as familiar as the stock characters in a TV sitcom. There's the precocious computer-savvy kid who can run rings around her elders, the skeptical old curmudgeon who is prone to saying "back in *my* day," and the know-it-all young IT professional burdened with supporting an office full of people who don't know a computer from a toaster oven. These stereotypes pervade our culture and influence our thinking about age, technology, and change. Like all stereotypes, they contain a kernel of truth—and, like all stereotypes, they can be deeply damaging if taken seriously as the basis for decisions affecting individuals or organizations.

This book is intended to help decision makers within organizations get beyond the stereotypes and better understand the relationship between generations and technology: where the differences in attitudes lie and where they come from, what they mean, and how the digital age gap can be bridged.

It's also a book about what happens next. Organizations derive their unique value from people. The living culture of the workplace is shaped not by impersonal economic forces, but by the values of the people who participate in it. Today, management and leadership positions are overwhelmingly filled by members of a demographic cohort whose

1

attitudes toward computers and technology—the essential tools of today's economy—were formed mostly in adulthood. Over the next 10 to 15 years, their roles will change, their influence will recede, and the next wave of leadership will be drawn from generations with remarkably different approaches to technology and workplace culture. Managing that transition in ways that empower rising workers without sacrificing the accumulated knowledge and wisdom of the veteran contributors is one of the crucial challenges facing businesses, governments, and society. Organizations will either find ways to blend the generations in harmony, or else face conflicts that threaten cultural continuity and productivity.

This issue is critically important as we move into the second decade of the 21st century. Because of the birth dearth of the 1960s and 1970s, most developed economies face gaps in the number of workers heading into the prime years of their careers. To sustain current levels of economic output, employers will need to rely on higher levels of workforce participation from older people, effective recruitment and retention of younger workers, and higher levels of productivity across the board. Increasingly, organizations will look to sophisticated new information technology (IT) tools to drive those higher levels of productivity.

Unlike previous waves of automation, which standardized rote processes and reduced manual labor, the technologies that power the knowledge economy touch on the most intimately *human* work activities: communication, collaboration, learning, leadership, decision making, personal reputation, and trust. The benefits they promise to organizations that adopt them are entirely dependent on people incorporating the new tools as an integral part of their work routines and embracing the profound changes they portend for people's relationships to information, organizational processes, and one another. Without the active cooperation of people in the workforce, deployments of these kinds of connected information work tools will not be successful.

Solving the generational puzzle is crucial to gaining necessary levels of cooperation from workers of all ages. Nearly two decades of scholarship has established the role that differences in generational attitudes play in all manner of social and workplace interactions. The three dominant cohorts in today's workforce—Baby Boomers (b. 1946–1962), Generation X (b. 1963–1980), and Millennials (b. 1981–2000)—exhibit fundamental differences in attitudes, priorities, values, and workstyles as a result of their different historical experiences, creating well-documented challenges for recruiters and managers.

Overlaid on the familiar lineup of generations is the *digital age gap*. Personal computers (PCs) first made their appearance in the late 1970s, and became mainstream work and consumer technology in the late 1980s. This demarcation cleaves the workforce into two distinct segments: those who saw a PC before they graduated from high school and those who did not. Generally speaking, all Millennials and most GenXers (especially those with elite educations) fall into the first group; nearly all Boomers and pre-Boomers fall into the second. This doesn't mean that all young people are tech wizards or that all older people are out of the loop—far from it. However, as we will see in later chapters, the point at which people have first contact with a computer, the Internet, mobile devices, and similar technology has profound implications for the way they learn and work in technology-mediated environments.

These differences interact with the other aspects of generational personality to make the implementation of certain kinds of collaboration and communication tools unexpectedly complex in the messy real world of human beings—to the undying frustration of results-oriented IT planners and strategists! Organizations may find that understanding and addressing *generational* differences rather than just *age* differences provides much more effective answers to the mysteries of why some technology solutions succeed and others do not.

The following two anecdotes illustrate the challenges and opportunities that can arise by recognizing, or failing to recognize, generational factors in people's approach to work and technology.

TECHNOLOGY AS THE LOCUS OF CONFLICT

An acquaintance of mine, Russ, recently described his experiences trying to facilitate a working group of faculty and administrators in a major American university. The group, composed of professors, researchers, assistant deans, and department heads (all Boomers), was charged with preparing some new policies for the employment of graduate teaching assistants. The group set up an e-mail listserv to enable discussions and collaborate on the documents it was expected to produce. However, the volume of communication exploded, and soon group members were receiving between 50 and 75 e-mails per day, often on matters as weighty as what snacks should be served at the next meeting. Collaborating on documents was even more problematic. Versions proliferated, people became confused and frustrated, and management became a nightmare.

Russ proposed setting up a collaborative Web site for the group, using a simple, low-cost hosted service accessible from any Internet connection. The space offered a document repository, threaded discussion groups, real-time communication via instant message and online meetings, contact management, and a shared calendar. Even in 2004, this was by no means new or innovative technology, and mastering the few simple techniques of the software did not seem beyond the capabilities of a group composed exclusively of people with PhDs.

Despite the manifest problems with the current system and the obvious benefits of the new capabilities, the group unanimously rejected Russ's proposed solution—by withholding their participation. Because hardly anyone used the site, it was not useful as a collaboration environment. The group cited the low level of utilization as a justification for their refusal to participate, and proudly clung to their dysfunctional e-mail system. Meanwhile, the committee's deliberations proceeded at a snail's pace, leaving important organizational issues unresolved and the disposition of hundreds of teaching positions (and research projects) in limbo.

If you take a purely mechanistic view of this situation, the behavior of the group makes no sense. Why would a group of extremely well-educated professionals choose to limit their efficiency and productivity by sticking with demonstrably inferior (and annoying) e-mail technology when a better choice was readily available?

Fortunately, what economists call the rational actor model is not the only tool of analysis available to us. The past 15 years have produced a rich assortment of studies on the distinct values and workstyles of the different generations. When these insights are applied to the scenario, a whole new layer of meaning is revealed. Indeed, the danger signs are everywhere. You have a group of highly skilled Boomer professionals accustomed to autonomy and control, whose power often stems directly from privileged access to information, suddenly being asked to share information out in the open. You have a group of high achievers, whose career success derives from recognition of their individual contributions, now forced to collaborate to produce an anonymous document for whose success they will receive little personal credit. And most of all, you have a group of prestigious subject-matter experts, who risk being exposed as incompetents if they prove unable to master an extremely basic (if unfamiliar) set of practices and technologies.

The social incentives for adoption of this technology are diametrically opposed to everything we know about the generational workstyle of Boomers. It challenges their need for implicit social hierarchies based on hidden knowledge and relationships, personal autonomy and expression, and status-based exemption from control and supervision. No promise of convenience or threat of sanction could overcome the strongly engrained biases that have governed their entire work experience. The dysfunctions of the old process are a small price to pay for the comfort it affords its participants.

It's equally certain that none of the participants would see the issue in those terms. If you asked them why they didn't want to use the workspace, they would probably reply that it was "too much trouble" or "I don't like to work that way." Because the group was unanimously composed of Boomers, these assertions would likely go unchallenged.

But consider for a moment if there were a few younger members of the committee—say, a tenure-track Assistant Professor in her mid-thirties and a graduate assistant in his early twenties. Instantly, the issues over adoption of the technology would become far more complex and contentious. Familiar generational conflicts over authority, management style, values, and outlook would surface in the context of the relatively trivial matter of how the group shares information in a networked environment. It is not difficult to imagine how this sort of dispute could inhibit group productivity even further.

The example of this university committee is a microcosm of the struggles taking place within and between organizations of all sizes, in all walks of life. In this case, the task revolved around team collaboration and document creation. In other cases, it involves finding and using information, incorporating data and business intelligence into strategic decisions, expanding the organization to reach out to partners and external resources, gathering and sharing knowledge, or creating new processes that simplify low-value tasks.

These knowledge-based activities—known hereafter as *connected information work*—are the building blocks of value creation in the knowledge economy. Customer service, new product and service development, sales and marketing, partnerships and supply relationships, and operational performance all depend on the ability of people to work effectively with information, processes, and one another. And increasingly, these activities are mediated by technology.

What the example shows is that it is not enough to say, "Here is our connected information work problem, here is a technology solution with the capabilities to solve the problem; therefore, we deploy the solution and our problem is solved!" This purely technocratic view lacks the power to explain or anticipate social and behavioral issues rooted in *generational* attitudes. Until organizations understand those kinds of issues well enough to address them through adjustments in practices and culture, they will encounter increasing difficulties in achieving the hoped-for benefits of their technology investments.

The inability to realize those benefits can lead to crippling disadvantages in speed, responsiveness, innovation, and insights. In the example, the unwillingness (and hence, inability) of the committee to solve its team collaboration problem with the best tools available led to a slower-than-necessary response to an important problem. Who knows how many opportunities the university lost to attract, retain, or promote the next generation of academic talent—the very essence of its value proposition—because it took months rather than weeks to develop a consistent policy in this area? How many other organizations will face critical challenges because of an inability to retain the knowledge of retiring workers, or bring customer information to bear on sales engagements, or use technology effectively in any of hundreds of other areas?

TECHNOLOGY AS THE ENABLER OF POTENTIAL

Prashant is a 21-year-old electrical engineering major at the University of Florida, working on a summer internship for a county government agency in western Washington. I interviewed him as part of my general research on the attitudes of Millennials toward various consumer and workplace technologies, but found that his story illustrates the larger advantages that organizations can experience by tapping into the exciting combination of technological savvy and entrepreneurial enthusiasm that the Millennial generation brings to the workforce.

As in many organizations, internships in the county government are vaguely defined and depend a lot on the skills, interests, and initiative of the intern, along with the willingness of the supervisor to support the intern's ambitions. Prashant presumably could have spent his summer making photocopies and sitting quietly in meetings. Instead, he decided to conduct a survey of project managers in the organization to determine the best methods of rationalizing two database systems currently used by the department, removing unnecessary fields that are not useful to managers, and optimizing the business rules to ensure more accurate and up-to-date data for future planning.

This project grew out of an earlier assignment simply to refresh information in the database. In the course of that work, Prashant observed that some information in the system was not connected to an actual organizational need or business requirement. "For example, we discovered that there was a requirement for project managers to file a monthly report, but it turns out that no one ever accessed these reports. They'd wait to see the quarterly ones instead," Prashant explains. "So why have that requirement when it's not useful? What I proposed is that we remove that task from the project managers and save them some time they could use on something else."

Did Prashant's supervisor devise this rather challenging assignment? Not exactly. "A lot of different projects that I'm involved in right now were not necessarily directed to me by my boss. I started out with one and ended up having so many questions that I would go to different people and then another project would evolve. For example, I am doing construction contract closeouts. I'm also doing research into sewer rates and sewer rate structures."

Prashant manages his time by alternating between his four highest-priority projects and setting deadlines for accomplishing particular tasks. This workstyle is self-directed, although Prashant expects and depends on frequent input from his manager. His engineering training and innate familiarity with computer technology allowed him to rapidly learn the technical skills he needed on the software, which gave him an opportunity to expand his role; his instincts for teamwork and consensus-building made it natural for him to solicit the necessary input from around the organization to build support for his efforts.

Prashant is a talented young man, but his skills and approach are not atypical of members of his generation. Observers of Millennials wax enthusiastic about their optimism, entrepreneurial spirit, ability to juggle a busy schedule, and desire to make a difference—characteristics not limited to the American-born members of this global generation. Prashant was born and raised in Nepal, but shortens the vast distance between himself and his friends and family with technology. He received what he describes as a typical education and rates his technical proficiency as a seven out of ten compared to his peers.

While the benefits of having someone like this as an employee might seem obvious, not all managers would be as indulgent of Prashant's entrepreneurial approach to his role, and not all IT departments would be comfortable with junior-level workers poking around at the business logic of a database. But government agencies in particular are likely to be hard-hit by retirements in the coming decade, and they will need to rely on the influx of motivated, talented, highly productive workers like Prashant to maintain continuity of service to their constituents. Consequently, the Boomer culture of the department was willing to accommodate the Millennial workstyle without imposing artificial management or technology constraints. What could have been a generational showdown over control, structure, access to information tools, and workstyles instead turned into a win-win situation for both the department and the intern—the kind of outcome organizations of any kind should hope for in managing across the digital age gap.

WHY SHOULD WE CARE ABOUT GENERATIONAL ATTITUDES TOWARD TECHNOLOGY?

These two examples are just the tip of a very large iceberg. The coming decades will see unprecedented demographic diversity in the workforce. Younger workers born after 1980 have grown up marinated in digital technology. It's integral to their workstyle and lifestyle, as are expectations of continuous change and challenge. Younger workers are always in demand for their up-to-date skills and lower labor costs relative to more established professionals. However, organizations that are socially or technologically ill-equipped to harness the talent of the Millennials will have difficulty attracting and retaining the skilled workers they need.

Older Boomers are nearing traditional retirement age, but their behavior is likely to be anything but traditional. Some Boomers may opt to wind down their working lives by transitioning out of high-pressure roles. The second decade of the 21st century is certain to see a continuing surge in the popularity of knowledge management as organizations scramble to document and retain the huge repository of skills, personal relationships, tacit knowledge, and cultural lore of their most senior workers before they walk out the door. Other Boomers (and pre-Boomers) may stick around well into their seventies and eighties, either out of choice or economic necessity. Many will be returning to the workforce or trying out new careers later in life. The social and technological requirements to enable the continued productivity of older workers are not only challenging in and of themselves, but are especially problematic if they must coexist with the vastly different practices necessary to motivate the Millennials.

Those who face the task of managing this change are likely to be younger Boomers or members of Generation X now heading into the prime of their working lives. As Generation X transitions into "Generation X-ecutive," they will need to find the right solutions to empower both younger and older workers, while retaining some semblance of governance over their organizations' IT infrastructure and costs.

When it comes to generations and technology, one size most certainly does not fit all. Generational issues around technology are largely unspoken and unacknowledged, but they can hamstring the efforts of organizations to get the most out of their investments in both people and information systems. Strategies that look good on paper may end up exposing underlying conflicts that paralyze productivity.

If an organization's most experienced professionals see new technology as a useless complication—or as a threat to their status and job security—even the best-designed systems won't produce expected returns on investment. Nearly two decades of failed knowledge management, customer relationship management, sales force automation, and portal-based solutions testify to the problems that occur when IT initiatives fail to account for people's everyday work habits, underlying attitudes, and the engrained culture of the business.

At the same time, if younger workers become frustrated with a slow-going approach that denies them the opportunity to use their skills or restricts access to the basic tools they know and use in their outside lives, they may take matters into their own hands by smuggling rogue applications into the enterprise, creating security, management, and compliance headaches for IT departments and the business as a whole. Or, worse, they may simply leave for greener pastures, taking their skills and energy with them.

In a world of increasingly complex and immediate challenges, organizations need to blend the knowledge and experience of older workers *and* the talent and enthusiasm of younger workers. Finding the answers to this dilemma begins by *starting a dialogue about technology across the generations.*

Younger workers' embrace of collaborative technology, such as social networks and instant messaging, isn't just about enthusiasm for the latest-and-greatest gadgets. These kinds of technology are an expression of their generational approach to problem solving and creativity. Organizations with foreknowledge about the attitudes and workstyles of their younger workers can begin making the adjustments and investments to capitalize on their skills immediately upon their arrival.

Likewise, the perceived resistance of older workers to innovation is neither inevitable nor insurmountable. Retirees who never learned or used computers in their working lives have taken to the Internet as enthusiastic "silver surfers" in increasing numbers. The cause of older workers' rejection or slow adoption of technology and technology-related practices often has more to do with sociological issues and workstyles than with the willingness or ability to learn later in life. An approach to training that accounts for these issues while imparting the necessary information at an appropriate pace can unlock the vast skills and experience of older workers in a context that allows organizations to effectively transmit and retain their knowledge using sophisticated technology.

Organizations can tap into the positive dynamics that drive technology adoption by aligning their practices, culture, and software strategy with the different expectations, motivations, and workstyles of all generations of workers. Training by itself is not enough, nor is overreliance on designed solutions that treat people as interchangeable parts in a static business process. Organizations should strive to understand how people work—individually, generationally, and within their roles—and optimize the technology to accommodate the widest range of options and the most diverse range of workstyles.

GENERATION BLEND

Organizations invest billions in connected information technology systems to keep up with the accelerating demands of the global economy, and billions more in recruiting and retaining top people to contribute leadership, ideas, and personal passion. So why not take a little additional time to ensure that people and technology are aligned to create productivity, not conflict?

This book offers some tools that managers can use to help identify where generational issues come into contact with connected information work technologies, and how to reduce the friction. The chapters in this book cover the following topics:

- Chapter 2, *Changing Workforce, Changing Work*, provides a strategic context for the discussion, focusing on the ways that demographic trends and technological innovation are transforming work and the workplace.

- Chapter 3, *Understanding the Generations*, presents an overview of generational analysis and its application to issues of work and technology.

- Chapter 4, *Older Workers: Blending Experience with Technology*, looks at the challenges facing the two oldest cohorts still in the workplace (members of the Silent Generation and the older end of the Baby Boom), and the factors in their unique workstyles that IT planners should consider to maximize the potential success of knowledge-retention efforts.

- Chapter 5, *Younger Workers: With Great Potential Comes Great Expectations*, puts the Millennial generation under the spotlight. What can organizations expect when the new kids on the block come charging into the workplace with their cutting-edge skills and sky-high expectations?

- Chapter 6, *Generation X-ecutive: Leadership from the Outside In*, focuses on midcareer workers—the younger Boomers and members of Generation X who are moving into management roles—and looks at how they are bringing their generational perspectives to technology decisions that affect the entire workforce.

- Chapter 7, *Reintegrating Older Workers into the Connected Information Workforce*, delves into the issues of technology training for older adults, exploring the successful approach of a New York–based organization that is helping to transcend the digital divide.

- Chapter 8, *Ambassadors of the Future: Turning to Younger Workers for Strategic Insights*, looks at Microsoft's Board of the Future program, an ambitious attempt to incorporate the views of Millennials into strategic planning efforts around the future of work and technology.

- Finally, Chapter 9, *Across the Digital Age Gap*, presents five issues for organizations to consider, along with some specific approaches to technology, work practices, and organizational culture that can help all generations use new information work tools to their fullest potential.

As new technology innovations continue to arrive in the market and in the workplace, organizations with cultures that accommodate generational diversity will enjoy an enormous competitive advantage. Organizations that can successfully blend the benefits of new technology with the natural skills of all their workers are more resilient to change, better able to capitalize on opportunities, and can offer a work experience that serves as a talent magnet for the best workers, whether they are 18 or 80.

~ 2 ~

Changing Workforce, Changing Work

The urgency of this topic arises from the convergence of two dynamics that are transforming the world in the first decades of the 21st century. The first is the generational shift underway across most of the developed world, as the cohort born after the end of World War II approaches retirement and a large new generation of Millennials prepares to make its mark on the world. The second is the increasing interpenetration of information and communication technology into all aspects of our lives.

Experts predict that the demographic shift will make it more difficult for employers to find skilled workers to fill critical jobs. The ubiquity of technology raises the bar even higher. It means workers will need to have deep knowledge of software, computers, and communication devices, even in jobs and industries that traditionally did not require those skills. With skills at a premium, employers will have less latitude to impose requirements by fiat or restrict hiring to only that narrow profile of workers whose approach to technology is ready-made to fit the priorities of the organization. Employers can use several tactics to cast a wider net for talent, but to do so, they need to be sure the technology they supply for their workers is intuitive, adaptable, and well-suited to the needs of a more generationally diverse workforce.

In this new world of work, sometimes the best person for the job will be a 70-year-old retrained manufacturing worker who needs to get quickly up the learning curve on Web content management software. Sometimes it will be a 24-year-old recent college graduate who has difficulty recognizing the boundaries between her freewheeling personal networking and communication style and the more regimented requirements of the workplace. A wise employer will find a way to unleash the talents of both, while managing around the differences in outlook and tech-savvy.

Generational differences in work attitudes are real, and technology can often be one more front in a continuous debate over conflicting values and priorities. The benefits of connected information technology are also real, and too important to the competitive performance of organizations to sacrifice on the altar of generational conflict.

THE LOOMING SKILLS SHORTAGE

How serious is the skills gap facing employers over the next 15 to 20 years? The numbers paint a stark picture across most of the developed world. The Baby Boom generation (b. 1946–1962), over 78 million strong in the United States, is nearing retirement age, potentially leaving a yawning gap in skills, leadership, knowledge, and experience. Members of the smaller succeeding cohort, Generation X (b. 1963–1980, when birthrates were lower), usually described as cynical, independent, and distrustful, are entering the stage of their careers where they become candidates for management and leadership positions. Behind them is another large generation of around 80 million Millennials[1] (b. 1981–2000, during a second baby boom in the United States), who have lived their entire lives surrounded and

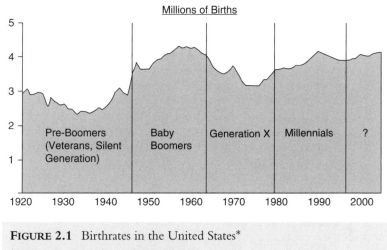

FIGURE 2.1 Birthrates in the United States*

Source: U.S. Bureau of Labor Statistics.

defined by information, technology, sophisticated expectations, and immediate feedback. Figure 2.1 shows the distribution of birthrates in the United States and the lines of demarcation between generations.

The decline in births between 1963 and 1980, and its slow return to near-postwar levels, created a gap in the numbers of working-age people entering the labor market during the 1980s and 1990s that will begin to make itself felt in earnest as the first wave of Boomers begins to retire in 2011. A widely quoted report from the U.S. Bureau of Labor Statistics estimated a shortfall of 10 million workers by 2010, based largely on the anticipated retirement of Boomers.[2] Throughout the second decade of the 21st century, the portion of the U.S. population under the age of 45 will shrink by 6 percent per year.[3] At the same time, the number of seniors continues to grow. By 2025, the U.S. population aged 65 or older will increase by 72 percent.[4]

The population pyramids shown in Figure 2.2 illustrate the changing distribution of the population by age and gender in the United States over the first four decades of the century. Note the increasing number of elderly at the top

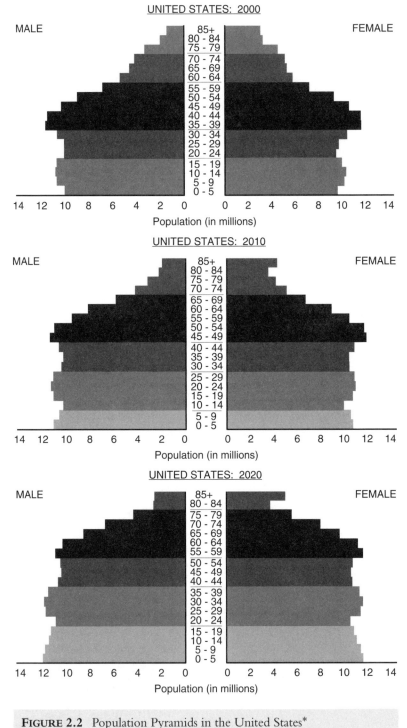

FIGURE 2.2 Population Pyramids in the United States*

*Source: U.S. Census Bureau, International Database.

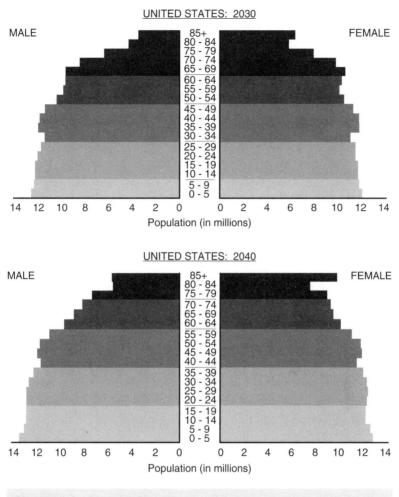

FIGURE 2.2 Continued

of the pyramid relative to the 30–50 cohort during the 2010s and 2020s, before the base begins to expand again. In other developed economies around the world, notably Japan and Western Europe, the aging effect is even more dramatic in the out-years because of a prolonged period of sub-replacement-level fertility rates. It is predicted, for example, that if current trends continue, in 2050, most adult Europeans will have no living relatives. As serious as the age gap and skills shortage are in the United States, they are much more significant in these countries, which will have to rely on large (and potentially disruptive) influxes of immigration and/or dramatic transformations of their political and economic institutions to meet the need for workers and satisfy their social obligations to the elderly.

The shortfall in raw numbers of replacement workers is exacerbated by the uneven distribution of skills and education in the post-Boom generations. Shortages of skilled workers are already acute in many industries, such as nursing and engineering. The median age of the workforce in public agencies and government is even higher than that of the private sector. A wave of retirements may carry away 60 to 70 percent of public-sector workers in the United States by 2012. Comparable trends will hit European and Asian governments as well.[5]

Ken Dychtwald, Tamara Erickson, and Robert Morison, in their 2006 book *Workforce Crisis*, summarize the problem this way:

> We have too few young workforce entrants to replace the *labor, skills, and talent* of boomer retirees. The more immediate loss is threatening the performances of many corporations. Since the generation after the boomers is much smaller, companies can no longer rely upon a relative profusion of younger workers. Even when they successfully hire and retain young workers, they are still trading experience for inexperience.[6] [emphasis in original]

Coping with a Graying Workforce

There are a few ways to reduce the impact of a labor crunch: (1) bring in more workers from somewhere else (immigration or guest worker programs); (2) send work to places where there are more people to do it (offshoring); (3) increase labor force participation (by attracting nontraditional workers, such as those beyond retirement age); (4) move workers from less productive to more productive jobs (training and retraining); or (5) reduce the demand for labor (automation).

The first two areas are out of the scope of this work, although they will probably continue to figure heavily in the plans of many organizations and countries. As for the last three, the skills gap appears to be severe enough to require at least some action on all fronts. Employers will simultaneously look to hire from outside the traditional labor pool, upskill and reskill existing employees, and drive higher productivity with new technologies. Chances are, technology investments will occur in areas affecting information workers and service professionals, because those are the areas where the potential for marginal efficiencies and increased value creation is the greatest, and where the skills gap is most keenly felt.[7] As for training, according to a report from the U.S. Bureau of Labor Statistics, 75 percent of the U.S. workforce will need to be retrained *just to keep their current jobs*—never mind those who aspire to move into positions that require new skills.

For this combination of measures to be effective, the capabilities of the workers have to keep up with the capabilities of the new tools and vice versa. The danger is that connected information technologies that support ordinary service jobs as well as specialized but non–computer–oriented professional work (such as healthcare or legal services) are becoming less accessible to those who lack the knowledge, comfort, and confidence to use them effectively, particularly older workers. And as we will see in Chapter 7, technology training programs are often not geared to the learning styles and generational values of older adults, causing many potentially valuable workers to abandon their efforts in frustration.

The skills gap is such that employers can't afford to give up on either older workers or the benefits of connected information work technology. But the gears have to mesh, and that means organizations need to look more closely at the intersection between generational factors and technology, with an eye toward closing the gap.

Increasing the Productivity of Information Work

Organizations invest in succeeding waves of new technology—and thus subject their workers to waves of changes in their lives and workstyles—to increase their productivity and competitiveness. Historically, productivity has increased when new technology replaced labor-intensive processes, first with mechanical machinery, and now electronic information systems. Over the past 40 years, large organizations have invested in enterprise IT solutions to increase the productivity of core business processes, from inventory and operations management to finance and accounting. These systems, which are often custom-developed to the needs of a specific industry, company, or process, excel in driving economies of scale into standard, repetitive tasks. They also provide management with deep, real-time visibility into operations, replacing the need for layers of lower-skilled workers and supervisors.

In service- and knowledge-based economies, the final frontier of productivity is *unstructured* information work: day-to-day tasks such as finding information, creating documents, preparing for a client presentation, finding the right person to answer a customer's question, organizing a meeting, or coordinating the efforts of a geographically dispersed team. Information workers in all roles, all organizations, and all industries perform these tasks dozens of times a day. Any little efficiencies that can save time and effort, or produce better results, are bound to add up quickly—provided that the enabling technology is broad-based and good practices can be adopted rapidly by people all across the organization.

Most unstructured information tasks are not considered high value in and of themselves, in that they are the work of almost any information worker, not just specialized experts. At the same time, they are nearly impossible to reduce to a top-down enterprise workflow process, because each instance of each task is unique and requires a different combination of skills, experience, and information. The issues that impact the productivity of groups working with information are things like locating relevant data that may reside in a number of different locations or formats, keeping track of document versions during a review process, making sure information is up to date, keeping management apprised of progress, and maintaining open communication— tasks that combine the capabilities of technology with the work habits of people. Technology at this level doesn't increase productivity by reducing the need for people: it increases qualitative outcomes by augmenting the skills and knowledge of the people already in place.

The role of people is critical. Author Jason Jennings persuasively argues that technology-driven efficiencies, even applied to high-level knowledge work, cannot alone provide a competitive advantage. He writes:

> Nothing counts, tracks, predicts and follows stuff better than technology, and eventually improvement in any of those areas theoretically reduces costs and results in improved productivity. But unless the software is proprietary—only one company has it—the same benefits can be achieved by every competitor. Consequently, no company can use the technology to achieve decided competitive advantage.[8]

Jennings defines true competitive advantage in the age of pervasive technology as "the ability to execute." Organizations that apply technology to their knowledge-dependent business processes in unique and interesting ways can gain a competitive advantage by empowering people to improve the quality of their processes. Hospitals don't measure success solely by the number of patients they treat, but by the number of good outcomes. The same is true in areas like customer service, new product development, and recruiting.

When people have access to the right information at the right moment, they are able to do *better* things, not just *more* things. There may also be cost savings in areas such as travel (reduced through remote collaboration), outside professional services (made redundant to the increased capabilities of employees), and risk exposure (reduced liability as a result of better control of internal processes), although these efficiencies are incidental compared to the increased ability of connected information work enterprises to create *new* value and capitalize on new business opportunities.

The great promise of new connected information work technologies—such as real-time collaboration, enterprise search, mashups, reputation systems, content subscription services, and other social computing applications—is that they provide access to vast resources of information in a context that is useful to people, without overwhelming them with too much random information. They serve as filters for complexity and a means for individuals to impose context and meaning on the maelstrom of data that surrounds them. Most interestingly, they are emergent: that is, the patterns of usage evolve naturally and adapt dynamically based on the needs of users and organizations, rather than following a rigid set of structured rules and practices. Writers like James Suroweicki (*The Wisdom of Crowds*)[9] and Don Tapscott and Anthony D. Williams (*Wikinomics*)[10] are just a few analysts who argue that collaborative content and broad-based distributed systems produce more reliable information that can result in better decisions, lower risk, and increased competitive advantage for organizations that adopt them.

The quantitative productivity benefits of these kinds of tools may be more difficult to measure, but that does not mean they are not real. Quality, not just cost, is what differentiates successful businesses from commodity providers. There will always be someone in a global market who can do the same thing cheaper, but there will not necessarily be anyone who can do it better. Service, innovation, brand strength, and quality provide the escape velocity for companies to assert pricing power and break the downward pull of commoditization. These factors depend on human talent and insight, amplified by a very specific set of technologies that make it faster, easier, and more convenient to connect with people, processes, and information to achieve business results.

Implementing these essential technologies and making them work as intended is not nearly as straightforward as retooling an assembly line. Not only is the technology richer in its capabilities, but the essential role of people in the creation of value makes the issues much more complex.

HOW TECHNOLOGY CHANGES WORK

Some technologies merely improve existing ways of working. Connected information work software *changes work*. The efficiencies that it adds to knowledge processes are significant enough to transform those processes beyond recognition. The immediacy of communication, collaboration, access to information, and visibility make practical entirely new modes of interaction among people, data, and structured workflows. Rich access to data through mobile devices, networks, and secure remote connections completely severs the bonds of time and place, and enables a radical reimagining of the workplace and workday.

The combination of connection and transparency both empower and expose workers in ways never before experienced in the workplace. Though people can acclimate to rising expectations and incremental innovation in the information environment, the totality and speed of the changes in the world of work are unprecedented, and can be profoundly disorienting—especially to older and retrained workers who are coming to the connected information environment from roles and occupations that moved to different rhythms. It is worth taking stock of the ways that technology has transformed work over the past two decades, as a way of tracing its trajectory forward and understanding the kinds of adaptations that work will demand of people and organizations in the 10 to 15 years ahead.

Technology Makes Work More Collaborative

E-mail and first-generation collaboration technologies became pervasive in the 1990s, but people, organizations, and software vendors struggled to find ways to integrate them smoothly into existing systems and ways of doing business. The ubiquity of connectivity even gave rise to a new problem of "information overload," where people struggled to dig out from under an avalanche of e-mails, meeting requests, context-free factoids, irrelevant search results, and constant interruptions. The ability to manage in this kind of information-rich environment is often cited as one of the critical differences in generational workstyles.

The bad news for overwhelmed workers is that the momentum for collaboration is growing even stronger. The good news is that the tools are getting better: more relevant, more contextual, less disruptive, and better integrated into the information work environment. Some of the most promising new information tools in the enterprise will seem very familiar to the (mostly younger) users of Blogger, LinkedIn, WikiPedia, Windows Live, Facebook, and other technologies currently grouped under the rubric Web 2.0.

More large organizations are beginning to see the utility of Web 2.0 technologies as tools for external communication and internal knowledge and content management. According to the industry trade publication *KM World*:

Corporations are using externally facing blogs for such functions as presenting commentaries about new products and responding to general inquiries from consumers. For example, the

Direct2Dell blog answers questions about XPS 700 computers and provides updates on Dell's battery recall. Although blogs are much less sophisticated than official corporate Web sites, they have an immediacy and interactivity that is hard to match using other approaches. Therefore, they are ideal for situations where a quick response is called for.[11]

A whole practice has developed around the promotion of blogging and other social networking applications in enterprise settings. Don Tapscott and Anthony Williams, authors of *Wikinomics*, confidently predict that wikis and collaborative content platforms will completely transform the process of innovation. They write:

> The lesson for business leaders is that the old monolithic multi-national that creates value in a closed hierarchical fashion is dead. Winning companies today have open and porous boundaries and compete by reaching outside their walls to harness external knowledge, resources, and capabilities. Rather than do everything internally, these companies set a context for innovation and then invite their customers, partners, and other third parties to co-create their products and services.[12]

A 2006 report on the use of new media in the enterprise by Edelman Change and Employee Engagement sums up the potential of "Enterprise 2.0":

> None of these new media technologies in and of themselves are truly innovative in terms of what they offer—blogs and wikis are simply easy-to-update Web sites and podcasting is merely a new way to transmit audio files. What has changed are the expectations individuals have of the ways they create, receive and share information. Today communications need to be relevant, interactive, portable and immediate. If organizations are not able to reach employees, or workers cannot access the information they want, when they want it, the result is likely to be a disengaged employee.[13]

According to several industry analysts, Web 2.0 collaboration, content management, communication, and collective intelligence applications are surging into the enterprise.

The question is: how will the different generations in the workplace manage the cultural adjustments necessary to adapt to a more collaborative, connected style of work?

Technology Collapses Time and Space

One of the most profound impacts of networked information and communication technology is the way it reduces—and potentially eliminates—the need for concepts such as the workplace and the workday. In many parts of the world, the penetration of high-speed networks and wireless telephony has reached 100 percent. Internet access is nearly ubiquitous (see Figure 2.3). Smaller, more powerful mobile devices offer the ability to connect to secure voice and data networks anywhere, anytime, and provide a high quality experience for accessing data, applications, and services.

Consequently, telework and remote access are increasing around the world. In 2005, 82.5 million workers worldwide did their jobs at home one day a month, more than double the figure from 2000, according to Gartner Inc., a technology research firm. Gartner predicts the figure will grow to more than 100 million workers by 2008.[14] In the United States, almost 29 million Americans now work remotely at least one day per month.[15] According to the research firm IDC, remote-access services are just now being recognized for their business continuity potential, and this market is expected to experience a year-to-year growth rate of 34 percent through 2010.[16]

Not every organizational role or worker is a good candidate for this workstyle. Many people benefit from or prefer the social environment of the workplace, and some organizations lack the culture, practices, and technology to ensure that work performed off-site meets quality or productivity goals without management supervision. There are

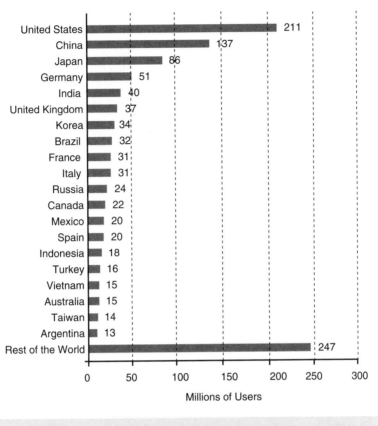

FIGURE 2.3 The Wired World, 2007

also management issues with telework—many of which are generational—that are impeding its progress, as discussed in Chapter 6.

As we will see, the promise of the distributed workplace means different things to workers of different ages and generations. Nevertheless, the rise of the distributed workplace has transformative implications for everyone. Older workers transitioning out of the workforce can stay in touch with colleagues, customers, and critical information without having to travel to the office. Midcareer workers can use the increased flexibility of work hours to balance work and life responsibilities, such as taking care of children or elderly parents. Younger people can leverage the global networks of friends and associates they have cultivated through their experience as students and consumers and bring their work experience into closer alignment with their life goals and expectations. But all of those things depend on people comfortably adopting the enabling technologies and integrating them smoothly into the way they live and work.

Technology Makes Work Transparent

A generation ago or less, if managers wanted real-time data about the performance of people or systems, they had to be physically present—on the shop floor, in a meeting room, on the job site, or at least in the corner office. Workers in most jobs had significant discretion simply because management couldn't be everywhere all the time.

Today, most large organizations use some form of enterprise information system to relay up-to-the-minute data on critical processes, such as Enterprise Resource Planning (ERP) systems in manufacturing, or Supply Chain Management to coordinate supply networks. But it goes deeper than that. Reports and other documents that were once stored away in file cabinets or saved on individual hard drives and floppy disks are now universally and persistently available on file shares, intranets, and perhaps the Internet. People can be reached instantly by mobile phone or text message, or asynchronously through e-mail, voice mail, task assignments, and collaborative workspaces. Emerging technologies can track and visualize relationships in the workplace by analyzing metadata from e-mail and collaboration systems. And the retention and protection of huge volumes of organization data is now mandatory as part of regulatory compliance regimes in many industries and many countries around the world.

Beyond the workplace, people leave footprints all over the Internet through their participation in blogs, social networks, online communities, and other activities. That information is visible not just to friends, but also to potential employers, colleagues, and business partners. As people-search technology improves, these fragments of identity will congeal into reputation profiles that can follow a person from place to place and job to job. Consulting firms are already establishing practices in reputation management to assist their clients with their aggregate online profiles.

The net result of these developments is that workers and their work product are more visible, accessible, and accountable than ever before. Whether you view this as a good thing or a bad thing probably depends on which side of the microscope you are sitting on; nevertheless, transparency is a fact of the 21st-century workplace.

Reactions to the transparent workplace vary considerably and correlate strongly to age. Older workers with experience are more likely to resent the lack of trust implied by ubiquitous monitoring and management of their work environment. Younger workers are less likely to take privacy for granted, but also less likely to care about being in strict compliance with organizational policies.

Technology Amplifies the Potential of People

Finally, current and emerging technologies give individuals and small teams the power to rapidly perform tasks that used to require vast numbers of people, specialized expertise, expensive equipment, and time-consuming processes. As connected information systems become smarter and more sophisticated, they will embed even more knowledge of processes and job-specific functions into the features of the software so that workers in generalized roles will have views into data that were previously the province of experts.

For example, the most recent versions of mainstream presentation and graphic design tools have incorporated solid modeling, three-dimensional rendering, and realistic lighting effects that, just a few years ago, required trained graphic designers using powerful workstations and complex software to achieve.[17] As a result, general analysts and ordinary information workers can visualize data in richer ways to gain or communicate deeper insights more quickly. In a few years, it would not be surprising to find that financial analysts, brokers, and day traders have access to advanced econometric modeling tools now running on supercomputers in central banks, accessible by a click from a menu in their standard desktop application suite.

The rapid advance of computing power, information work software, and networks cuts a swath of turbulence through the information workplace. On one hand, it drives increasingly sophisticated insights and analytic abilities from the bureaucratic center to the edge of the organization, where they can influence front-line, customer-facing processes, product development, supply relationships, and day-to-day management decisions in real time. On the other hand, it pushes exceptional responsibility and competence onto the shoulders of workers in nonexpert and nonmanagement roles. Workers who want to stay employable are therefore under constant pressure to master new skills and new tools that give them an advantage in finding the information they need.

The ubiquity and accessibility of data in information systems tends to devalue the knowledge that people carry around in their heads, which in turn affects generational power relationships in the workplace. Today's younger workers are often criticized for not knowing as much as their older colleagues. They don't read as much, and likely received less fundamental preparation in domain-specific subject matter from their education. Studies bear this out. What younger workers know is how to find information they need when they need it, using search engines, social networks, data visualization applications, and person-to-person communication tools—a skill that one of my colleagues calls "just-in-time comprehension." When the workplace provides them access to these facilities, younger workers have no problem substituting the ability to find and apply data for innate knowledge. Eventually, they gain experience of their own, which they then share with other peers when asked. Networked technology enables networked learning, and supports the collaborative orientation that Millennials bring with them as a by-product of their cultural experience.

The educational system is only starting to come to grips with this tectonic shift away from linear learning and toward the more networked model. Evidence shows that young people often receive better training in 21st-century work craft from their experience as consumers in the wired world than they do from formal instruction in schools and universities. The implications of this will be explored more fully in Chapter 5. In the meantime, older and midcareer workers, who came into the workforce under a much different set of conditions and expectations, have neither the formal preparation nor the continuous exposure to the connected world that younger people do. Organizations looking to older workers as a potential solution to the coming skills shortage need to consider the different ways that older adults from the predigital generations learn and use new technologies, and the unique barriers they may face compared to their younger colleagues.

DISRUPTIVE IMPACTS OF TECHNOLOGY

For organizations to realize the most far-reaching benefits of new and emerging technology, they need people to embrace change at an extraordinarily deep and disruptive level.

Without a coordinated strategy to address the implications of new technology on personal workstyle, team dynamics, and organizational culture, management risks squandering not only its investments in new software and systems, but also the skills and morale of its workforce.

Software Complexity Restricts the Talent Pool

There's usually a trade-off in the design of new technology devices and software between capabilities and usability. Gadgets and programs that do a lot of stuff can be difficult to use. Attempts to reduce the complexity to users through abstract and apparently simple interface metaphors can have what author Edward Tenner calls "recomplicating effects"[18]—that is, the metaphor becomes more complicated than the thing it is trying to simplify. As software seeks to integrate more capabilities and reach deeper into job- and role-specific functions, the tools can become increasingly difficult for nonspecialists to learn and use. At a certain point, learning the software becomes a job in itself, divorced from the real-life skills that are typically associated with doing good work. Software design guru Alan Cooper describes the situation this way:

> The obnoxious behavior and obscure interaction that software based products exhibit is institutionalizing what I call "software apartheid," where otherwise normal people are forbidden from entering the job market and participating in society because they cannot use computers effectively.[19]

Tools that are overly complex can therefore artificially limit the potential pool of workers—exactly the opposite outcome that employers desire when facing a shortage in the overall number of people to fill key jobs.

Consider this example of an occupation that was utterly transformed by technological innovation. A generation ago, industrial designers worked in clay or other tactile media, then translated their designs into hand-drafted sketches. It stands to reason that if you have a talent for envisioning solid objects, shapes, and surfaces, natural media offer the most intuitive means of expression. When solid-modeling computer-aided design (CAD) systems began appearing on affordable workstation hardware in the 1980s, the entire design profession had to rethink its approach to its craft in order to accommodate the enormous and undeniable efficiencies of digital technology.

A designer who is accustomed to thinking the way a CAD system works can produce work every bit as good as one who sculpts, draws, or assembles models using traditional media—with the additional advantage that the CAD plans can be put immediately into review and production. But using a CAD system demands an extremely different approach to the creative process. A visual thinker needs to learn how to translate his or her ideas into the language of the software—a cognitive leap that is by no means easy or natural for someone whose expertise (and perhaps interests) lie elsewhere.

Eventually, the relevant industries solved the problems of migrating traditional designers to computer-based systems. Some workers made the transition by acquiring the necessary skills, either at their own expense or that of their employer. Some left the business. Special accommodations were made for extremely valuable or senior people who continued to work using their own techniques. Schools and training programs began teaching CAD systems as part of the basic design curriculum. On one hand, this helped ensure that the next generation of designers would already have internalized the approach preferred by their future employers. On the other hand, it probably weeded out those who may have had a talent and vision for design, but lacked the patience and/or aptitude for *computer-based* design.

CAD systems are highly specialized and complicated pieces of software, built to be used by experts in well-defined job roles. However, the example is illustrative because current and future generations of mainstream connected information work applications are nearly as rich and complex in their own way as CAD systems, and the value they create is just as critical to the competitiveness of organizations that use them. A suite of information work tools might include not just the standard word processor, spreadsheet, presentation maker, and e-mail client applications, but also software to enable collaboration, real-time communication, information management, search, subscription-based services, workflow design, form design, project management, Web site design, visualization of business data, and many other functions. The information tools that today's high school students will use in their jobs on a day-to-day basis probably have not been invented yet. Organizations looking for truly differentiated levels of value creation will need their workers to not just know but *master* highly sophisticated suites of knowledge tools and integrate their use deeply into their work routines.

An office worker in a nontechnical role, such as a marketing manager, financial analyst, project coordinator, or quality assurance manager, may therefore need to internalize a large body of purely *software skills* to participate fully in ordinary day-to-day activities like meetings, task assignments, and document reviews. Knowledge of specialized software was rarely a precondition for success in these jobs before, but it will increasingly be so in the future. This has significant implications when a generationally diverse workforce brings such disparate views, styles, and expectations of technology to the workplace.

Complexity Increases Specialization and Isolation

Problems of complexity and specialization arise because organizations typically deploy new technology solutions tactically and opportunistically to address particular sets of issues. Human Resources, for example, may build a portal to allow employees to track their vacation time and 401(k) performance; Finance may build its own portal to enable expense reporting over the Intranet. Each of these applications may appear to solve a particular problem in an elegant, "best-of-breed" way. They may even leverage a common IT infrastructure to reduce technical support and development costs, and thus appear to comply with good governance practices.

From a people perspective, the proliferation of customized solutions built on different technologies, different data repositories, and different design principles creates a huge overhead of complexity. That's not necessarily a decisive barrier in the short run. Sophisticated applications often work well on their own terms and drive considerable efficiencies into the practices they are intended to optimize. People can be trained to use this or that application. Eventually, they become proficient in it, to the point that their proficiency shapes the way they do their job. As an unintended consequence of this process, boundaries between tasks, roles, and disciplines within the organization harden because they are each supported by systems and practices whose design differences emphasize an artificial degree of specialization. Compartmentalization is reinforced when data is siloed in underlying IT systems that do not communicate or interoperate effectively.

The rigidity implicit in this approach to IT runs counter to the long-term interests of organizations, which will soon be faced with titanic challenges in attracting, retaining, and cultivating skilled workers. Jobs that require too much *custom* software knowledge can be difficult to fill, making the costs of workforce turnover painfully high from a recruitment and training perspective. Younger workers wary of getting locked into low-value roles or who are oriented toward building a useful skills portfolio for a long, multifaceted career may find little appeal in spending months gaining proficiency on a system that has no wider application beyond a very specific job, activity, or employer.

Technology Can Create Perverse Incentives

The deployment of complex technology in a general business setting can send mixed messages to workers about what's really important, putting personal motivation at odds with organizational objectives.

Technology can create opportunities for younger, less-established workers who can quickly master software-related skills, or whose workstyles are already in sync with the capabilities of the connected business environment. Proficiency with software may lead to false perceptions of competence in job areas that require intrinsic subject-matter expertise or experience. Customer service representatives, for example, may have extensive training in their customer relationship management (CRM) and Knowledge-Based systems, yet know next to nothing about what it takes to actually improve customer satisfaction. Managers can become masters of spreadsheets and project flowcharts with no insight into team dynamics, motivation, or communication. When IT elbows its way into the center of business processes, it can end up creating specialized roles with no particular value beyond mastery of software and related processes.

For otherwise-valuable workers who see technology as extrinsic rather than central to their jobs, this creates all kinds of added pressures. They not only need to adjust their workstyle to fit different ways of doing business and different measures of success, but they must also do so in competition with other workers who have no conceptual bridges to cross in terms of using new tools and techniques. Jennifer Deal, who conducted extensive surveys on generational attitudes about a variety of workplace issues in her 2006 book *Retiring the Generation Gap*, discovered a fairly significant divide on this subject. She writes:

> Although this problem [technology change] was reported by people of all generations, it was mentioned far more frequently by older respondents. They pointed out that they hadn't grown up with computers as their younger colleagues had and that the constant small changes in technology were wearing. They said they understood why the changes were necessary and that they really tried to keep up, but that it just took a lot of time and was frustrating to them. Younger people didn't talk about the issue in the same way. Some mentioned that constant technology changes were often as irritating as they were helpful. Others said they enjoyed keeping up on the newest and best options when it came to technological improvements in their work.[20]

When seniority correlates with clout, as it often does in organizations, this can cause big conflicts. Senior workers with the most to contribute and the most influence over decisions are the ones most irritated by technology improvements designed to capture and share *their* knowledge across the organization. Annoyance over the technology, combined, perhaps, with deeper concerns about the implications of collaboration and transparency on their work and status in general, can hinder successful implementation of the very programs organizations need most to avoid knowledge and productivity loss.

Even workers who are willing to share knowledge and participate fully in communities of practice, knowledge bases, and documentation projects find the supporting technology too difficult to integrate into their existing workstyle. Knowledge-sharing tasks may be recognized as *important* but not *urgent*. If knowledge-capture tools are too cumbersome and intrusive, knowledge sharing will remain perpetually on the to-do list of busy workers and never actually get done.

OUTLOOK

Organizations can improve the chances of success in driving real improvements in productivity and value creation by taking generational issues into account in planning for technology deployments. Fortunately, there is a large body of work devoted to understanding and managing generations in the workplace. The next chapter presents a summary of the literature to date, with special attention to observations relating to technology attitudes.

ENDNOTES

1. With immigration, there may be as many as 90 million Millennials in the U.S. labor market by 2020, according to the U.S. Census Bureau.

2. Fullerton, Howard N. Jr., and Mitra Toossi. *Labor Force Projections to 2010: Steady Growth and Changing Composition.* U.S. Bureau of Labor Statistics, 2001. Note that these estimates were later revised downward as a result of immigration, productivity gains, and workforce participation rates.

3. Gordon, Edward. *The 2010 Meltdown.* Westport: Greenwood Publishing, 2004.

4. According to the U.S. Census Bureau.

5. An excellent discussion of these issues and their policy implications. See Longman, Philip. *The Empty Cradle: How Falling Birthrates Threaten World Prosperity [and What to Do About It].* New York: Basic Books, 2004.

6. Dychtwald, Ken, et al. *Workforce Crisis: How to Beat the Coming Shortage of Skills and Talent.* Boston: Harvard Business School Press, 2006, p. 12.

7. According to Dychtwald et al., "by 2010, 25 percent of all workers will be in professional occupations, the most information intensive of all." *Op. Cit.* p. 11.

8. Jennings, Jason. *Less Is More: How Great Companies Use Productivity as a Competitive Tool in Business.* New York: Portfolio, 2002.

9. Surowiecki, James. *The Wisdom of Crowds.* New York: Anchor Books, 2005.

10. Tapscott, Don, and Anthony Williams. *Wikinomics: How Mass Collaboration Changes Everything.* New York: Portfolio/Penguin, 2006.

11. Lamont, Judith. "Blogs and Wikis—Ready for Prime Time." *KM World*, January 1, 2007.

12. Tapscott, Dan, and Anthony Williams. "Innovation in the Age of Mass Collaboration." *Business Week*, February 1, 2007.

13. "New Frontiers in Employee Communications, 2006." Edelman Change and Employee Engagement/PeopleMetrics, 2006. www. edelman.com/image/insights/content/NewFrontiers2006_ Final-paper.pdf.

14. Rhoads, Christopher, and Sara Silver. "Working at Home Gets Easier." *Wall Street Journal,* December 29, 2005.

15. Amble, Brian. "US Sees Big Rise in Teleworking" *Management Issues*, February 13, 2007.

16. "Remote Access Services to Grow at 34% a Year." ITFacts Software, September 1, 2006. www.itfacts.biz

17. And these capabilities are getting better all the time. See Greene, Kate. "Animation for the Masses—Adobe Is Creating Software to Let Home Users Create Movie-quality 3D Graphics." *MIT Technology Review*, September 5, 2007. www.technologyreview.com/Infotech/19344/?a=f

18. Tenner, Edward. *Why Things Bite Back: Technology and the Revenge of Unintended Consequences.* New York: Vintage, 1996.

19. Cooper, Alan. *The Inmates Are Running the Asylum. Why High Tech Products Drive Us Crazy and How to Restore the Sanity.* Indianapolis: SAMS/Macmillan, 1999.

20. Deal, Jennifer. *Retiring the Generation Gap: How Employees Young and Old Can Find Common Ground.* San Francisco: Jossey-Bass/Wiley, 2006.

~ 3 ~

Understanding the Generations

In a country as diverse as the United States, people in the same general age group may have precious little in common. Is it useful or appropriate to generalize about demographic cohorts as large as 80 million strong, and to use those generalizations as the basis for important business decisions? A growing body of literature from sociologists, business analysts, and management consultants argues that, in fact, it is.

LIFE STAGES AND GENERATIONS

Before getting too far on this subject, let's address a potential point of confusion. The term *generation* is sometimes used interchangeably with the idea of *life stage*. That is, the "younger generation" is anyone who happens to be under 30 at the present moment, as distinct from the "older generation"—those closer to retirement. That's certainly one way to look at the age gap. Young people just starting out have different priorities and different habits than those in midcareer angling for advancement or those at career peaks later in life, and those differences are important to consider. However, it would be wrong to assert that today's under-30s behave the same as the under-30 cohort of 1990 or 1970. It's observably the case that these cohorts exhibited genuine, profound differences at equivalent stages of life, and have developed in different directions as they matured.

The term *generation*, then, is used here to identify birth cohort, not life stage. Consider Baby Boomers, a generation currently heading toward the far end of midlife. Despite their best efforts, Boomers are no longer the free-spirited adolescents or yuppie go-getters that they were in their twenties and thirties. They are now leaders, members of the establishment, even grandparents—the very things many of them defined themselves in opposition to earlier in life. It is not surprising that they now act very differently than they did when they made their first appearance in American history, yet they remain identifiably distinct compared to the generations that preceded and followed them. Boomers as elders are still Boomers in the way they see the world. They may learn new things, and they may change their political views, fashions, or tax brackets, but their basic outlook remains constant.

One of the main theoretical underpinnings of this book is that, although the priorities of different generations change along with their life stage, people maintain their fundamental generational values, formed by shared historical experience, as they move through life. Most members of Generation X, for example, have moved out of their twenties and are now starting families, but the priorities they are setting for themselves entering midcareer are very different from those of Boomer moms and dads just 10 or 15 years ago. Millennials, despite some superficial similarities with their immediate elders, will pose different challenges to employers and offer different opportunities than GenXers. As young workers, they still want to establish themselves and put their skills into practice—same as every generation newly arrived in the workforce—but their generational style in doing so will mark them as distinct, as will their approach to parenthood, midcareer, and mature leadership when they reach those stages.

Organizations that plan for the future assuming that today's midcareer workers will be motivated by the same factors and exhibit the same behavior as the early Boomers did 15 or 20 years ago might be in for a surprise. Those who are able to adapt to the different styles of the generations in their roles, however, are likely to be well-positioned to attract, retain, and maximize their return on people. Given the integral role of technology today, understanding generational attitudes in the context of life stages and job roles is a fairly important exercise.

As of now, 2007, there are three-and-a-half generations in the workplace, distributed over three life stages (or, in this context, career stages). Figure 3.1 shows the overlap of generations and life stages.

Chapters 4 through 6 address the generations in the context of their current career stages. Chapter 4 deals with older workers, and thus discusses both the oldest Boomers and the remaining members of the Silent Generation still in the workforce. Chapter 5 looks at the unique issues facing younger workers, primarily Millennials. Chapter 6 deals with midcareer workers soon to emerge as the next cohort of organizational leaders: currently, younger Boomers and the leading edge of Generation X.

FIGURE 3.1 Life Stages and Generations

Life/Career Stage		Young Workers	Midcareer/ Emerging Leader	Career Peak
Generation	Millennials	GenX	Young Boomers, Older Boomers	Silent
Ages in 2007:	Under 26	27–44	45–61	62+

GENERATIONAL ANALYSIS AS A FORECASTING METHODOLOGY

William Strauss and Neil Howe introduced the idea of generational personalities into modern discourse with their 1991 book *Generations: The History of America's Future, 1584–2069*.[1] In it, the authors developed a methodology for assessing, explaining, and forecasting the ways that generational factors influence the events of historical eras. According to Strauss and Howe, the alignment of generational types at different stages of life produces a predictable cycle of social dynamics that has replicated itself several times over the course of American history from Colonial times to the present.

Generations was widely acclaimed at the time of its publication and has become one of those books that is so influential that it disappears from sight as a specific piece of scholarship. However, anyone inclined to dismiss generational analysis as a fad or a shopworn cliché should reread Strauss and Howe's Chapter 13, "Completing the Millennial Cycle" (particularly about how Boomers would treat their first elected President in the event of a moral lapse, and the likely response of Boomer leadership to a terrorist attack that the authors expected to occur sometime at the beginning of the 21st century), and compare it to any futurist writing from the same time. Clearly, Strauss and Howe discovered something important, and their methods have become popular because they have robust predictive and explanatory power.

Since 1991, others have applied the methods of generational analysis to management and produced a myriad of recommendations for attracting, retaining, motivating, and understanding workers of different age groups. Don Tapscott, in *Growing Up Digital*[2] (1998), was among the first to apply these insights in the area of technology. These insights can be helpful in addressing the underlying causes of many types of misunderstandings and miscommunications that hamper productivity.

Insights into the behavior and values of generations can be especially useful in understanding attitudes toward technology, because technology innovations, like other epoch-making events, are linked to discrete moments in time. Boomers famously recall when they first heard President Kennedy had been shot, or that Neil Armstrong had taken the first human steps on the moon. GenXers may recall when they heard of the *Challenger* disaster, the fall of the Berlin Wall, or the death of Kurt Cobain. For Millennials, it was September 11, 2001. These big events, all analysts agree, helped shape their common generational experience.

Each generation's first encounter with computers and technology may have been less memorable but at least as significant. I recall when the first Apple II appeared in my seventh-grade classroom. I was old enough to understand its novelty, but too young to appreciate why some people might find the little beige box intimidating. It was just a cool, interesting new thing, and my friends and I went about learning to use it with the enthusiasm, resourcefulness, and competitive spirit typical of boys that age. From that point on, I tended to view computers as tools for getting things done more quickly and easily, rather than as fearsomely complicated and mysterious boxes. The technology evolved in a way that made sense to me based on my understanding of how computers worked and what they could and could not do. The marketing talked to me directly as a target consumer. The design choices appealed to my aesthetics, and new programs seemed easy to learn because they built on skills and knowledge I already had.

As I grew older, I discovered this experience was fairly common to people of my generation (Generation X), and that I share a general set of attitudes with my peers that form the baseline set of assumptions that underlie any discussion of technology. I also quickly discovered that those attitudes were not common across all age groups. I still remember my confusion when my uncle, a professional writer from the Veteran generation, was not immediately excited by the possibilities of the AppleWriter word processor. How, my younger self wondered, could anyone possibly prefer the mess and fuss of typewriter ribbons and whiteout to the elegant convenience of the Delete key? "I just like what I know," he said. "It will take me longer to figure out the computer than the time it will save me." His reaction, alas, was reminiscent of my own when I was first introduced to MySpace a couple of years ago. "So what?" I thought. "Who needs a crazy-looking Web site to keep track of 'friends' I've never met?" He eventually came to terms with word processors, and I set up a (rudimentary) MySpace site, but I suspect I can relate to his sense of being slightly out of his element.

GENERATION VS. GENERALIZATION: A FEW CAVEATS

Both analytic and anecdotal evidence shows there is value in trying to explain the attitudes of individuals and groups according to their generational outlook. But as with any broad approach, there are bound to be exceptions. The attitudes of individuals are shaped by personal experience as well as collective historical events. When people become aware of theories that try to describe them as part of a trend, at least a few will consciously adjust their behavior to disprove the theory or will object on principle to being stereotyped. I anticipate that at least a few readers of all generations will react strongly to one thing or another in this book as completely foreign to their own experience and attitudes. To them I offer apologies. My intention is not to contribute to ageist stereotypes, but to help expose underlying causes of friction that people and organizations can address to make their experience with technology less stressful and more productive. I hope that even disagreements with the specific conclusions reached here can lead to better discussions and a better understanding of age-related factors in technology adoption.

Generational outlook is also just one of many cross-cutting social factors that influence attitudes. Good books can and should be written on the effects of gender, economic class, educational attainment, ethnicity, and nationality on people's outlook toward technology, to help organizations and technology vendors understand the implicit biases that may exist within current approaches to product design, training, and implementation. The fact that this book looks at generational attitudes should not be read to suggest that this is the *only* possible framework or even necessarily the best one for looking at the issues, which are too important to be limited to a single dimension of analysis.

Finally, I should note that a few of the people and sources with whom I consulted in the course of my research did not support this book's thesis and expressed well-reasoned skepticism about the relevance of age to this topic. For example, Jennifer Deal's excellent 2006 book, *Retiring the Generation Gap: How Young and Old Can Find Common Ground*,[3] presents compelling evidence that the different generations in the workforce have remarkably similar attitudes toward a wide range of issues, but have different ways of expressing them. Several other writers and analysts I spoke with point out that attitudes toward technology can be seen as a subset of attitudes toward complexity and change, which are primarily matters of individual temperament, economic background, education, and occupational expertise, or the results of specific design features of different products.

I don't disagree with these perspectives. However, I would point out that one critical way that technology differs from more general social and organizational issues is that messages about technology are deeply and deliberately segregated by age. The high-tech industry makes a conscious effort to associate its products with the excitement of youth in highly visible marketing campaigns. Younger people have been targeted as consumers since the 1980s, with messages promoting the benefits and downplaying the troublesome aspects of computers, software, devices, data services, high-speed connectivity, and literally thousands of specialized, highly complex products. The messages are keyed to generational sensibilities and reference cultural touchstones that have specific, emotionally resonant significance to younger customers. At the same time, media coverage of computers and the Internet—especially in newspaper features and TV newscasts disproportionally consumed and trusted by older audiences—often focuses in a sensationalistic way on the failures, risks, and problems of technology (e.g., viruses, identity theft, online sexual predators). It is no surprise that perceptions of technology can vary significantly among the generations.

High-tech marketing for enterprise systems, including office productivity software, is usually targeted at the IT or business decision makers, not the end users. Most information workers are not party to the discussions of business and technical benefits surrounding new workplace technologies. When people are presented with a new piece of technology to integrate into their work practices, they are influenced less by the business-value marketing claims of the vendors and more by the generationally-based attitudes they bring with them to work as a result of their experiences as consumers, students, and citizens. These attitudes can help determine whether they will embrace the technology and make it work, or reject it.

Some products are so well-designed and well-integrated that resistance is not an issue, even for less technologically sophisticated workers. They are easy to use; their value is immediately apparent. People of all ages love them, use them, and trumpet their virtues from the mountaintops. Likewise, some people can learn and use almost anything quickly, or else can't be trained at all; they are early adopters or laggards by nature, not by age or any other external factor.

In these cases of unusually excellent technology or wizard users, critics are right to say that age and generational outlook have limited predictive value, and we should look to other reasons why deployments succeed or fail. But in the vast middle ground, where most real-world technology and most ordinary users struggle to accommodate one another, generational issues can play a role. At the least, understanding the influence of generational attitudes can help organizations with a lot at stake mitigate the risks of change and accommodate the diversity of responses to technology that will doubtless occur in an intergenerational workforce.

WHAT IS A GENERATIONAL ATTITUDE?

One of the guiding principles of generational analysis is that each cohort's basic values and outlooks are shaped by shared historical experiences. Boomers, for example, were made aware of their importance from the moment of their birth, as the engines of robust consumerism in a society recovering from nearly two decades of war and depression. In the 1960s, they pushed against cultural barriers and found that they gave way—their ideals really *could* change the society they lived in, if not the entire world. Not every Boomer interpreted those experiences in the same way. In the United States, debate over the legacy of the 1960s still hangs over the politics of the early 21st century, and the most bitter partisans on both sides are almost all Boomers.

Analysts likewise attribute the cynicism and self-reliance of Generation Xers to their relatively small numbers and historical circumstance of growing up in an era when institutions had proven themselves bankrupt. Independence, distrust of authority, and pragmatism (in contrast to the high-flown idealism of the Boomers) were and remain a rational response to the situation that many GenXers found themselves in, growing up in an era of shrinking expectations and promiscuous superficiality.

In the workplace, the traces left by history manifest as distinct values, habits, communication styles, motivations, and attitudes. They affect everything from work ethic to fashion sense. Whether or not individual people see themselves self-consciously as members of a generation, the methods of generational analysis produce convincing explanations for the behavior of workers of different ages in common situations, and, according to the authors of the many books on the subject, have helped organizations of all kinds address otherwise-vexing people problems in the workplace.

For the purposes of this study, the important question about the generational attitudes observed by these writers and experts is: "How do these attitudes affect the ways that workers of different ages participate in a deeply connected information workplace?" This question has implications for the management of both people and technology as organizations look for ways to maximize productivity in the midst of a skills shortage.

This is not quite as simple as asking "How do people of different ages use computers?" although that is one facet of the issue. Generational analysts often label younger generations as more tech-savvy than their elders, because they were raised and educated around computers and networks in ways that Boomers and pre-Boomers were not. Generation Xers and Millennials both started their careers with more basic knowledge of technology, which not only helped them contribute immediate value in certain kinds of tasks, but also gave them confidence that they had skills that some of their more senior colleagues and managers lacked.

Older workers who came of age in the predigital era can and do become as proficient in technology as GenXers and Millennials, but the barriers are higher. Older workers have more at stake because they are often well-established in their organizations and roles, while nagged by constant concerns that they are a step behind younger people in their comfort level with new technology (concerns that are reinforced by media messages and new products aimed exclusively at younger consumers). They may also perceive implications to new technology that younger managers may miss because of their different generational outlook, but they don't know how to express their objections because they are not as comfortable participating in discussions about technology.

These problems can be solved by recognizing the importance of distinct generational attitudes as part of the organizational approach to technology. In Chapter 7, the older adults learning computers for the first time may represent an extreme example of inexperience that is not as common in the mainstream working world anymore, but the general practices employed in the training have broad applicability because they were designed to address generational differences in learning style that many younger managers simply do not consider. Of special interest is the intergenerational component, where older adults share wisdom and insights with youth in exchange for the kind of supervised, step-by-step training that is necessary to get them comfortable with new technology.

This kind of dynamic demonstrates that initial generational attitudes toward technology evolve through experiences and interrelationships. They are not simple or predictive, and they can be changed through effective management and open communication.

GENERATIONAL ATTITUDES AND WORKSTYLES

The term "workstyle" refers to the various habits, practices, and preferences that people have toward the way they do different parts of their job. Some people prefer phone and voice communication; some prefer e-mail; some use text messages. Some managers want constant updates on project status, whereas others only judge results and leave process details to their subordinates. For some people, face-to-face meetings are an indispensable opportunity for networking, team building, and knowledge transfer; for others, they are a waste of time.

Workstyle also pertains to the way people express their personal values through work. Is it more important, for example, to provide accurate information in a crisp, terse way or to offer a warm, friendly interaction? Is a handshake worth more than a contract? Is management obliged to explain the reasons for its decisions? Is it appropriate (or sensible) to expect organizations to reciprocate employee loyalty?

Because workstyle is an outgrowth of the larger values and expectations that people bring with them to their jobs, it is an area where generational outlook leads to some real differences in behavior based on age cohort. Most generational analysts have a lot to say on generational workstyles. For example, in *Generations at Work* (2000), authors Ron Zemke, Claire Raines, and Bob Filipczak provide thumbnail sketches of the workplace personalities of the different generations, based on their research and consultancy experience.[4]

Figure 3.2 necessarily simplifies and abbreviates the well-supported set of observations explained in depth in *Generations at Work*. It is also based on data that is now more than seven years old—a passage of time that has mitigated some of the issues regarding the experience levels of

FIGURE 3.2 Generational Attributes*

Boomer	Generation X	Millennial ("Nexters")
Core Values: • Optimism • Team orientation • Personal gratification • Health and wellness • Personal growth • Youth • Work • Involvement	**Core Values:** • Diversity • Thinking globally • Balance • Technoliteracy • Fun • Informality • Self-reliance • Pragmatism	**Core Values:** • Optimism • Civic duty • Confidence • Achievement • Sociability • Morality • Street smarts • Diversity
Assets: • Service oriented • Driven • Willing to go the extra mile • Good at relationships • Want to please • Good team players	**Assets:** • Adaptable • Technoliterate • Independent • Unintimidated by authority • Creative	**Assets:** • Collective action • Optimism • Tenacity • Heroic spirit • Multitasking capabilities • Technological savvy
Liabilities: • Not naturally budget minded • Uncomfortable with conflict • Reluctant to go against peers • May put process ahead of results • Overly sensitive to feedback • Judgmental of those who see things differently • Self-centered	**Liabilities:** • Impatient • Poor people skills • Inexperienced • Cynical	**Liabilities:** • Need for supervision and structure • Inexperience, particularly with handling difficult people issues

*Summarized from *Generations at Work: Managing the Clash of Veterans, Boomers, Xers and Nexters in Your Workplace*. By Ron Zemke, Claire Raines, and Bob Filipczak. AMACOM/American Management Association, 2000.

FIGURE 3.3 Generational Workstyle Matrix

Workstyle issue	Boomer	Generation X	Millennial
Motivation – why they work	• Gain status through achievement • Personal impact • Save for impending retirement	• Enable lifestyle • Realize creative or entrepreneurial vision • Economic security and independence	• Make social impact • Satisfy high expectations • Learning and personal development
Trust and transparency	• Trusts philosophies and ideologies, not institutions • Expects that commitments will be honored	• Distrusts authority • Wants proof • Skeptical of commitments	• Trusts parents, teachers, and guiding figures • Sees popularity as validation • Wants to hear the big picture
Management style	• Interpersonal, team-oriented • Politics and unspoken relationships important • Command-and-control, hierarchical	• Individualistic, results-oriented • Less attached to process • Impatient with structure	• Insufficient evidence
Communication style	• Self-consciously inclusive, politically correct • Indirect and euphemistic • Sees value in packaged communications	• Informal, sometimes abrupt • Values authenticity over sparing feelings • Distrusts slogans and buzzwords	• Eager to please, conflict-averse • Inclusive by nature • Content of communication less important than act of communicating

FIGURE 3.4 Generational Technology Workstyles

Workstyle issue	Boomer	Generation X	Millennial
Collaboration and autonomy	• Peer consensus valued • Smooth team dynamics prioritized over efficiency	• Prefers to work independently • Teamwork is opportunistic and results-oriented, not an end unto itself	• Collaborative by nature • Values networks as problem-solving tool
Need for feedback and supervision	• Takes initiative • Prefers feedback through formal channels • Wants recognition for personal achievement	• Wants to be judged on work outputs, not appearances • Wants explanations and justifications from management • Needs effective management to maintain morale	• Thrives on continuous feedback • Prefers structured assignments • Needs to see strategic or social value in work
Work/Life balance	• Workaholic legacy, but now seeking more balance • Reluctant to forego status conferred by work; wants to stay relevant and active • May have increasing responsibilities to children, aging parents, grandchildren	• Works to live, prioritizes lifestyle over career choices • May be tempted into higher levels or engagements as leadership opportunities open up and financial responsibilities increase • Many are now starting families and will prioritize time with kids	• Accustomed to multitasking; work is just one more thing to fit into the schedule • Looks for work opportunities that advance personal development goals and social values

(Continues)

FIGURE 3.4 (Continued)

Issues	Boomer	Generation X	Millennial
What information and communication technology represents	• Instrument for improving personal productivity • Transactional source of information • Something new to learn • Indicator for status • Manifestation of organizational approach to solving a business problem	• Instrument for saving time and effort • Interactive way to connect with people and information • Something new to figure out, master, and find the limitations of • Gadget to enhance lifestyle or work experience	• Default way to think and work • Instrument for building, sustaining, and participating in networks • The inevitable next cool thing • The way any organization manages operations in the modern world
Concerns about technology in the workplace	• Too difficult and complicated to learn and use • Reduces personal value by socializing private knowledge and relationships • Reduces perceived status by reducing autonomy and discretion • Adds a new and unfamiliar criterion for success	• Imposes unwelcome overhead of process with no apparent value • Gives management too much control and visibility, indicating distrust of worker • Raises privacy concerns • Doesn't work properly or isn't implemented right	• Limits creativity and collaboration because of usage restrictions or missing features • Is not as vivid or responsive as technology they are used to • Specialized tool takes time to learn and has no relevance to future career path

GenXers and Millennials, which the authors have addressed in subsequent works. The point is that these generational traits, which are similar to those observed by other analysts, have tangible implications for the way that people of different ages work, manage, and lead. Figure 3.3 summarizes the findings of various writers on generational attitudes on some key issues related to workstyle. Figure 3.4 applies those attitudes toward technology in particular.

OUTLOOK

The next three chapters will delve deeper into the characteristic priorities and workstyles of each generation and look at how connected information work technology has the potential to amplify, transform, or disrupt work in the next 5 to 15 years. Organizations that understand these underlying dynamics stand a much greater chance of successfully blending generational workstyles with technological innovation to achieve the kind of outcomes they expect.

ENDNOTES

1. Strauss, William, and Neil Howe. *Generations: A History of America's Future, 1584–2069*. New York: Vintage, 1991.

2. Tapscott, Don. *Growing Up Digital: The Rise of the Net Generation*. McGraw-Hill, 1998.

3. Deal, Jennifer. *Retiring the Generation Gap: How Employees Young and Old Can Find Common Ground*. Center for Creative Leadership/ Jossey-Bass (an imprint of John Wiley & Sons), 2006.

4. Zemke, Ron, Claire Raines, and Bob Filipczak. *Generations at Work: Managing the Clash of Veterans, Boomers, Xers and Nexters in Your Workplace*. AMACOM/American Management Association, 2000.

~4~

Older Workers: Blending Experience with Technology

In the 1930s, the U.S. government set the retirement age for collecting Social Security benefits at 65, which was, co-incidentally or not, the average life span of an adult male at the time. Americans born in those days are just now entering their seventies and showing no signs of slowing down. Advances in medicine and lifestyles are helping people live longer, healthier lives. Many seniors are prolonging their physical health and mental acuity by staying active in their communities and jobs. As the most prosperous generation in American history—perhaps in human history—most don't *need* to continue working, but their lives have been defined by their contributions to civic institutions, and many enjoy the opportunity to remain engaged at some level.

The current crop of genteel, civic-minded seniors is just a warm-up for the graying society's main event—the impending transition of the forever-young Baby Boomers into full-blown elders. By every indication, they will not go quietly. Idealistic, hard-working, quarrelsome, and in endless need of attention, Boomers are likely to transform old age the way they have transformed every other social institution they have touched.

Boomers currently make up 45 percent of the U.S. workforce,[1] and many will continue working well beyond age 65, both out of desire and economic necessity. For employers, this is a welcome development in an economy where skills are at a premium and younger workers are suspected of lacking the Boomers' commitment to organizational objectives. Organizations can capitalize on older workers' skills and proven work ethic to add maturity, stability, strongly rooted values, wisdom, and know-how for competitive advantage. Organizations also have an urgent need to preserve the knowledge and skills of their incumbent senior workers. Those assets contribute untold value, and they can be lost for the price of a farewell luncheon and a gold watch.

Technology plays a critical role in both amplifying and preserving the knowledge of older workers, but older workers have the most problematic relationship with knowledge and collaboration tools. Elite first-wave Boomers have long been muscular proponents of change—technological and otherwise—and they now realize, sometimes to their regret, that they must live by their own rules to keep their place in the workforce. Those who have not been immersed in the culture of technology can find the costs of entry into new careers painfully high. Some Boomers also perceive new collaborative content and distributed decision-making technologies as a threat to their hard-won authority.

Organizations have a lot to gain if they can overcome these challenges. Extending the careers of productive workers beyond retirement age can offset some of the costs of training and recruitment, while keeping important knowledge and relationships in place. Blogs, wikis, and other collaborative content applications can make it easier to collect and share the knowledge of experienced workers—if they can be persuaded to contribute. Telework and mobile access can keep older workers engaged in the workplace without the daily grind of the traditional workday—if those workers and their supervisors can get past the "presenteeism" mindset that equates productivity with attendance.

To clear these hurdles, we must first understand the real problems. In the case of older workers, it's not enough to ascribe difficulties with new technology to fear of change or stereotypes of elders being set in their ways. Evidence shows that older adults can be avid and eager adopters of almost any new technology under the right conditions. Instead, organizations should look to the underlying effects of new technology on the issues central to the specific values, workstyle, and priorities of Silents and Boomers, as those are likely to be the biggest barriers to adoption.

THE SILENT GENERATION

When we talk about older workers in the workforce, we're actually talking about portions of two different generational cohorts. The most senior workers still participating in significant numbers are those born during the Great Depression and before the end of World War II (1925–1945)—younger than the Veteran generation that actually served in the War, but quite distinct in outlook from both their older siblings and the Boomers that followed. Strauss and Howe call this the Silent Generation and discuss their distinct attributes at some length. There are also many people from the first wave of the Baby Boom, starting in 1946 and going through the mid-1950s, who differ in most ways from the Silents but share some of their attitudes toward technology because they were well into their careers by the time personal computers made their appearance.

Silents are the oldest generation in the workforce, mostly there by choice, though economic necessity sometimes plays a part. They were the first—and possibly last—generation to enjoy the fruits of defined-benefit pension plans, fully funded Social Security and Medicare benefits in the United States, and the savings accumulated from a lifetime of thrift, instilled by the formative experience of the Great Depression. As such, 95 percent have formally retired and are collecting some form of pension benefits or Social Security.[2] In 2005, they comprised approximately 8 percent of the working population.

Many of this cohort who retired from their first careers have opted to extend their working lives by starting businesses, trying out new occupations (such as teaching), volunteering, or increasing their participation in community or political groups. About 68 percent of all of today's workers say they plan to work in some capacity even after they retire.[3] The behavior of Silents in elderhood is setting the stage for Boomers, who may prolong their working lives out of choice or necessity in greater numbers. Boomers who reach age 65 in 2011 can expect to live, on average, at least another 18 years.[4]

Throughout their working lives, Silents distinguished themselves through their methodical, diligent work habits, often in service of a vision of persistent, progressive social evolution. Strauss and Howe describe them variously as "technocrats" and "helpmates,"[5] but in fact their cultural legacy is far more disruptive and revolutionary than that of the Veterans or the Boomers. Silents were at the vanguard of changes later credited to Boomers, such as the Civil Rights movement, the sexual revolution, feminism, and consumer advocacy. They transformed the culture and contributed to the flowering of American arts and letters in the latter 20th century. Martin Luther King, Jr., Robert Kennedy, Bob Dylan, Gloria Steinem, Cesar Chavez, Ralph Nader, and Hugh Hefner are or were all members of this generation, as are Senator John McCain and business tycoon Warren Buffett. In management, the Silents' legacy is the tolerant workplace that did away with formal barriers and discrimination, and values consistency of process over personal bias. They also presided over the globalization of business that began in the 1990s and continues to accelerate today. Conversations with people of this age often reveal a continued desire to contribute, both as workers and as citizens, and a faith in the value of institutional culture that has become increasingly rare.

Workers in their sixties and seventies not only have the potential to remain productive, thanks to increasing life spans and health improvements, but are also the custodians of irreplaceable knowledge, relationships, and cultural lore. Silents are managers and incrementalists by nature, with a strong sense of fairness and an increasingly rare ability to analyze information objectively and deeply. Even those who spent most of their careers in operational or service roles possess information and insights that can help organizations solve practical problems that might frustrate less experienced managers. Those returning to the workforce or continuing in their roles bring values of patience, linear analysis, and historical context that are found far less frequently in younger workers—and which, in fact, many organizations would dearly like to impart to members of later generations.

Silents are the most likely generation to have avoided digital technology in their work and lives. Even the youngest were well into their careers when general-purpose computers appeared in the workplace, and older still when they became affordable as consumer devices. Many Silents express an initial fear or reluctance to experiment with technology. They prefer to learn the "right way" to do what they need to do from detailed manuals or authoritative classroom instructors. They approach technology with curiosity, openness, and humility. Once they figure it out, however, they are among the most eager to use it to express their talents and insights.

Even the most robust members of the Silent Generation will only be in the workforce for another 10 to 15 years. However, as the number of younger workers (and younger *skilled* workers) declines and organizations look to elders to fill, or continue in, significant roles, the practices developed today for the retention and management of Silents in their senior years may play an important part in the human resource strategies of organizations looking to hold on to more numerous Boomer workers and retain the value of their knowledge, skills, and experience.

OLDER BOOMERS

From a demographic perspective, it is possible to view the Baby Boom as a monolithic phenomenon, extending from the return of the troops from World War II (1946) to the introduction of the birth control pill in the United States (1962), after which the birthrate declined precipitously. Many similarities extend across this entire cohort from the oldest to the youngest, in contrast to traits exhibited by Generation Xers born just a few years later. At this particular moment in history, however, important sociological distinctions can be made between those born in the early years of the Boom and those born from the mid-50s onward. The latter group, now in their mid-forties to early fifties, have more in common from a technology attitude perspective with older GenXers than they do with their fellow Boomers born before, say, 1955. In fact, many of those responsible for the PC revolution in the 1970s and 80s were second-wave Boomers. As such, they will be discussed in detail in Chapter 6, *Generation X-ecutive*, dealing with midcareer workers just now moving into leadership roles, rather than this chapter, which addresses issues particularly affecting workers past their mid-fifties.

The first flush of the Baby Boom generation, born 1946 to 1955, was shaped by a radically different social, economic, and political environment than the Silents, and it shows in their generational personality. *Patient* and *methodical* are not adjectives often applied to Boomers, whose most senior cohort includes Bill Clinton and Hillary Rodham Clinton, George W. Bush, Donald Trump, Steven Spielberg, and Oprah Winfrey. This generation was groomed from birth for leadership and success. They were raised in an era of affluence, rising expectations, and increasing technological progress—balanced by the unprecedented threat of nuclear annihilation and the global confrontation with Communism.

The leading edge of the Baby Boom marched through life with a sense of certainty and entitlement. They tended to view the great issues of their day—Civil Rights, the Vietnam War, the role of women, the power of government—in terms of moral absolutes. Though they did not trust institutions as the Veterans and Silents did, older Boomers have always been big believers in ideas, even if their personal behavior tends to fall short of the high truths that govern their lives. Boomers' enthusiasm for ideas has led them to embrace succeeding waves of theories promising radical transformation (of oneself, business, or society), sometimes leading to a management strategy that Zemke, Raines, and Filipczak characterize as "management by buzzword."[6] As idealists and big thinkers, Boomers often tend to prefer bold all-or-nothing strategies rather than patient incrementalism.

Older Boomers today are at or nearing their career peaks in their mid-fifties and early sixties. Many are in positions of leadership, which they may have occupied for a decade or more. According to a survey of the 2,500 largest publicly traded corporations by Delaware management consultancy Booz Allen Hamilton, CEOs in the United States are entering offices at younger ages. In 1995, the average starting age of a CEO was 50.4 years; in 2001, it dropped down to 48.8. High-tech executives are younger still. An information technology CEO is only 45.2 years old on average; in telecommunications, the average is 45.7 years. The oldest CEOs upon taking office are those in the materials services (53.7 years) and the utilities sector (52.5 years).[7]

The personal styles and values of Boomer CEOs set the tone for the organizational culture, and their view of the world defines the strategic priorities of their organizations. Accustomed to being the center of attention since birth and putting in long hours to earn their stripes, many older Boomers will prefer to remain in positions of power and authority rather than withdraw into retirement. Lynne Lancaster and David Stillman, in their book *When Generations Collide* (2002), observe that many Boomers "tend to view retirement not as a well-earned rest, but with ambivalence, even discomfort."[8]

Some Boomers will change careers or rejoin the workforce later in life motivated by a commitment, belief, and desire for self-actualization. Thirty-five percent of America's Boomers said lyrics from the Beatles song "The Long and Winding Road" most closely resembled their vision of retirement, while 8 percent said the lyric "I hope I die before I get old" best describes their vision. "They absolutely reject the idea of retirement. They're going to work until they die," said Myril Axelrod, a New York City marketing consultant who has studied Boomer attitudes.[9]

Some are in career tracks such as teaching, government work, or physical labor that offer strong incentives for workers to transition out after a fixed term of service or upon reaching a certain point in life, even when many productive years may still lay ahead. Some have seen grown children leave the nest and want to resume careers or interests that were put on hold while raising families.

Even those who wish to retire may be unable to do so. Fewer than one Boomer in six has sufficient savings to finance a comfortable retirement, and many would face extreme and unfamiliar hardships by moving to a fixed-income lifestyle. A recent study conducted by UBS in the United States found that 77 percent of respondents expect to engage in part-time work during retirement, either to earn a major or a minor supplement to retirement income, up from 70 percent 10 years ago.[10] Roughly 25 percent of Boomers have saved nothing for retirement, and 43 percent of Americans say they will have to reenter the workforce almost as soon as they leave it.[11] Eight in ten Boomers plan to work at least part-time during their retirement. Only 16 percent say they do not expect to work at all.[12]

This surfeit of senior workers could be a boon to employers. Callaway Partners cofounder Tony Rich, quoted in the *Christian Science Monitor* in May 2007, cites the benefits of hiring those over age 50. In addition to their broad experience, he says, "The work ethic they bring is just incredible. They come from a generation that grew up working hard and doing whatever it takes."[13]

Older Boomers will continue to provide the benefits that employers have depended on them for over the course of their productive careers. They are, and are likely to remain, one of the best-educated generations in American history, producing a bumper crop of professionals with advanced degrees (28 percent have a bachelor's degree or higher)[14] now reinforced with long job experience and personal maturity. Self-starters and change agents, older Boomers work well without extensive supervision and internalize the values of their organizations to a far greater extent than do their younger counterparts. They value high achievement as an end unto itself, and their desire for peer consensus helps give cohesion to organizational cultures.

"They bring experience, and with that comes better judgment, better productivity and better customer service," said Stephanie Klein, president of The Boomer Group. "What company doesn't need those attributes?"[15]

GROWING UP PRE-DIGITAL

Virtually the only similarity in the generational profiles of Silents and older Boomers is in their approach to information technology. Both cohorts were well-established in the workplace when PCs began making their appearance in the 1980s. Prior to that time, computers were the tools of specialists: complex and inaccessible pieces of industrial equipment housed in their own glassed-in data centers, serviced by a priesthood of data management professionals, computer scientists, engineers, and technicians. Significantly, these IT jobs were considered support roles, distinct and disconnected from the center of decision-making authority. Only the outputs of computer systems, not the computers themselves, found their way into the hands of business managers, in the form of reports, printouts, and responses to transactional queries. It was not only unnecessary for most nonspecialists to become too familiar with the details of data-driven processes, but it was in some ways a level of detail unbecoming of an executive.

The first-generation PCs that ran office applications were likewise often restricted to administrative and clerical staff. Proficiency with a word processor or a presentation design program was neither useful nor socially desirable for higher-level managers and professionals. Also, many men of this age never learned to touch-type and found keyboard-based input slow and inconvenient. Desktop computers looked and behaved like fancy typewriters; they posed little compelling interest to many midcareer professionals.

By the 1990s, the increasing capabilities of technology, the arrival of younger, more tech-savvy workers, and the elimination of many administrative support positions in waves of downsizing created a much broader user base for PCs in the workplace. Between 1990 and 1994, PC sales in the United States went from 16 million to more than 37 million, compared to only 40,000 sold in 1976 (mostly to young Boomer hobbyists and engineers). By 2004, there were 173 million PCs sold worldwide.[16]

PCs became easier to use with graphical interfaces and what-you-see-is-what-you-get (WYSIWYG) applications.

E-mail, file sharing, and the first generation of collaboration technologies began to take hold, along with better ways to connect individual workers to large enterprise data systems. This, in conjunction with falling costs of hardware, vastly increased the value of technology in many aspects of work and led to its broader adoption.

Veteran-era workers with less inclination to learn new skills late in life took the arrival of computers as an opportunity to retire. Those with similar disposition but more clout were able to insulate themselves from direct contact with computers by delegating that sort of work to younger subordinates. Older executives often had expensive computers on their desks, which they bragged to colleagues about never using. Some rising Boomers who aspired to their status emulated their example by affecting a personal disdain for technology (even if they advocated its use elsewhere in the business).

In some cases, high-tech devices appealed to Boomers as objects and status symbols. Having the best computer or the best mobile phone was a visible manifestation of prestige, irrespective of the utility of the technology to their actual work. So, for a variety of reasons, many Boomer professionals were early adopters of PCs as they were establishing themselves in the 1980s. They continue to be heavy consumers of technologies like mobile telephony and e-mail, which support those aspects of the Boomer workstyle that rely on communication, networking, and keeping one another in the loop through personal contacts. Industries such as media and advertising, communication, and high-tech, which employ large numbers of Boomers, have long been on the cutting edge of technology. The competitive Boomer work ethic, a by-product of being part of a generation of nearly 80 million, also plays a part in motivating middle-aged workers, who might otherwise be content with some stability in their working lives, to keep up with the rapid pace of change driven by constant innovation.

Among large organizations of all types today, there are relatively few areas where PCs and connected information work technology have not penetrated at least a little bit. To people whose current roles are now defined by their inboxes and Blackberries, it is difficult to imagine anyone under 60 who has not acquired at least some basic computer skills in the course of their working lives. However, even into the 2000s, it was possible for experienced, highly educated professionals in various occupations and industries to avoid having much to do with PCs, the Internet, office productivity software, and even e-mail. We will meet some of those people in Chapter 7, which discusses ways to integrate older workers with limited computer experience into a connected information work environment quickly and effectively.

Even high-achieving, well-connected older Boomers feel some stress about the relentless, rapid pace of change and the requirement to keep technology skills continuously up to date. It is a perfectly natural and understandable reaction for a senior professional who has spent 30 years keeping current with successive waves of computerization and connectivity to eventually make a stand and say "this far and no farther!" Like the Boomer-dominated faculty committee in the example in Chapter 1, these professionals would rather make do with technology whose faults they have learned to tolerate than go through yet another cycle of change and adaptation. However, powerful as the Boomers are in terms of cultural and economic clout, they can't stop the flywheel of constant innovation, driven by relentless global competition. Boomers, as leaders and individual contributors in their organizations, face the same edict that they offered the generations before them: adapt or get out of the way.

At this late date, it may be tempting for employers—especially those from younger generational cohorts—to dismiss older adults who gave up on the high-tech treadmill, or perhaps missed the computer revolution entirely, as irredeemably old-fashioned, intransigent, or slow-witted.

That view is not only unkind and shortsighted but also fundamentally incorrect. The coming skills crunch makes it impossible for organizations, governments, and society to disregard the potential contributions of the relatively large numbers of older workers—both early Boomers and Silents—who are still willing and able to participate in the workforce. Furthermore, evidence convincingly demonstrates that older adults can become both proficient and comfortable with sophisticated computer technology, so long as the training program recognizes the underlying social and conceptual barriers unique to older workers and finds good ways to address them.

TECHNOLOGY ISSUES FACING OLDER WORKERS

Older workers are not inherently technophobic and demonstrate no gaps in their overall aptitude to learn and master new technologies. On the contrary, evidence suggests that older people are avid and enthusiastic to learn new skills of all kinds and use new technology to enrich their lives. A 2005 study sponsored by the Society for Industrial and Organizational Psychology (SIOP) found that the older workers they observed were actually *more* receptive to change than their younger peers. SIOP reports that, "Analyses show that older employees report higher affective commitment than younger workers, showing belief in and desire to see the implementation occur."[17]

Seniors today account for the majority of new Internet users; more than 32 percent of all Americans older than age 65 are now online and regularly use e-mail and other forms of digital communication.[18] As we will see in Chapter 7, older adults with no prior experience with computers and profound concerns about their ability to learn can be successfully given both skills and confidence with the right training approach.

So if older people are smart, resourceful, competitive, and motivated, and the new tools aren't that difficult to learn, then what accounts for the observable age gap in adoption of useful collaborative and information-sharing technology within organizations? For that, managers and strategists need to look at what the technology does, rather than how it works.

Many of the innovative Web 2.0–based applications that organizations hope will enable broader capture, retention, and dissemination of knowledge are designed by technocratic GenX, Millennial, and young Boomer software developers and deployed by ambitious GenXer-run IT staffs, who are completely unmindful of the ways they trespass on sensitive issues at the core of older Boomer and Silent Generation values and workstyles. The resistance they encounter is not necessarily a reaction to the shortcomings of the technology, but to the deeper changes that older workers must integrate into their tried-and-true methods for success.

Can you blame them for being reluctant? They perceive, either consciously or unconsciously, the ways that technology innovations impact their unique ability to add value, challenge long-held beliefs and practices, reduce their control of their work and career, and influence the way they are seen by colleagues, superiors, and subordinates. For these people—often the most senior and knowledgeable in the organization—the personal risk/reward ratio looks considerably different than it does to the technocratic strategist.

Technology Can Put Older Workers at a Competitive Disadvantage

Older workers are familiar with—and largely comfortable with—command-and-control hierarchy as the organizing principle of management. Boomers may have distrusted authority in their youth, but they have grown quite comfortable exercising it in fairly traditional ways once they ascended into leadership roles, despite efforts to appear more humane and open-minded than the authoritarian Veteran bosses for whom they worked. Zemke, Raines, and Filipczak characterize the Boomer leadership style as "collegial, consensual, sometimes benignly despotic."[19]

In Boomer-led organizations, the real centers of power may not be obvious on the organization chart, but they are clearly demarked by complex behaviors and political machinations that participants have learned to recognize. Competition is real and cutthroat, since the number of Boomers competing for resources has always been so large. Power stems not only from control of information, access, and relationships, but also from the ability to conceal its exercise under a blanket of gracious inclusiveness, omnicompetence, and concern for the common good.

In this context, any display of weakness can open the door to a competitive challenge to authority. Older workers recognize that they are at a disadvantage in learning new technology compared with younger people, who internalized digital skills at a much earlier age. Each time some new technology requirement is layered onto an existing process, it creates both complexity and risk. Even when a new technology promises improvement to an existing process or some long-hoped-for convenience, there is great incentive for older workers to conceal their discomfort and lack of confidence behind face-saving objections, lest their imagined inability to keep pace with younger peers be exposed.

If this dynamic goes unacknowledged, it makes it difficult or impossible for older workers, especially those in positions of authority, to take advantage of special training programs or to reach out to younger colleagues for help: the last thing they want is to be singled out. Besides, many older workers know from firsthand experience with

younger family members that it is not always easy to get
patient, straightforward answers about how computers and
digital equipment work.

Discomfort with Technology Creates Anxiety

One of the most common concerns voiced by older workers
about new technology is that they might break something
if they don't operate it properly. "I was concerned that I
would screw up a computer by pushing the wrong buttons,
and, yes, I did have that fear," admits Beverly Daffner, a
retired teacher with several advanced degrees, who has since
become much more comfortable with her PC.[20]

This fear can easily be reinforced by coworkers or impatient helpmates who provide assistance without explaining
what they are doing, or who access deep, expert-level features of the device or software to fix the problem. For many
older workers, it is easier to rely on younger colleagues and
subordinates than learn the software themselves. This strategy may work for awhile, but it leaves the older worker ill-
prepared for later changes in career or lifestyle, and makes
the learning curve that much steeper when it becomes necessary to learn new technology themselves.

These common scenarios can reinforce an older
worker's sense of incompetence and uncertainty. They
demonstrate that new technology represent a forbidding
degree of complexity, and that younger people are simply
better wired to understand it than they are. People in this
downward spiral of confidence become easily frustrated and
impatient with change, and begin to believe that they lack
the ability to learn new skills. Combined with other negative messages that society sends about aging, this attitude
can significantly diminish a worker's productive capacity
and morale, creating a self-fulfilling prophesy of career ob-
solescence.

Bottom-up Content Networks Invert Authority

Certain types of connected information technologies and practices pose an even greater challenge to cherished values of Boomers and Silents. Both cohorts of older workers vest great credibility in information from authoritative sources. Silents were raised in an era of less cultural diversity, when strong institutions propagated linear narratives of history that neither accounted for the perspectives of outsiders nor apologized for that omission. To them, information needs to be institutionally validated in order to be trustworthy. In interviews, Silents are most skeptical about the reliability of data in user-created repositories, the most reticent about providing personal information online, and exhibit the most initial confusion about concepts related to collaborative content development.

The views of first-wave Boomers were shaped by different factors. Part of a gigantic generation that emphasized sharing and caring as affirmative values, Boomers learned the value of concealing natural self-interest beneath a cloak of inclusive, team-oriented rhetoric. Many figured out that hoarding information could be an effective strategy to exert control in a group setting without pulling rank or making other overt demonstrations of power that Boomers find distasteful. They were also, from birth, test subjects for the most vivid and seductive one-way communication technology ever developed: television. The top-down flow of information from a centrally controlled production and distribution center is part of their natural experience, much more so than the idea of a bottom-up network of content contributors.

Finally, Boomers grew up during a time defined by high-stakes ideological conflict and internalized a dualistic view of the world that they have applied, in widely disparate ways, to personal, spiritual, political, social, and work-related issues for their entire lives. Boomers have chosen sides since childhood, from the great debates on the shape of politics and society (e.g., Civil Rights, Vietnam, women's rights, big government vs. small government, Clintonians vs. Neo-Conservatives) to the fads and fashions of their own lives, and the sides they embraced helped shape their world-view and identity. Consequently, the ideological context of information—its source, the motives for publishing it, the conclusions it supports (or challenges), its implications—are often critical factors in helping Boomers ascertain whether to commit their trust. Information presented without clues to its source can be disorienting:"What if I agree with this analysis, and then find out that it undermines my ideological position or betrays my political loyalties?" or "Why should I trust that information if I don't know why I need to pay attention to the person who wrote it?"

In top-down information environments, that is not a problem because the source and authority of information is evident and can be either accepted or not, depending on your values and loyalties. But in decentralized, bottom-up networks, it can be far more difficult to keep loyalties and ideologies consistent.

Objectively speaking, organizations and leaders operating in a dynamic, competitive environment would seem to have an interest in grinding down the rough spots caused by ideological or politically motivated adherence to low-performing strategies. That's rarely the case in the real world, where leaders and teams routinely become emotionally invested in their positions and fear losing authority by allowing contrary data to alter their stated course of action.

By and large, Generation Xers and Millennials tend to take a more instrumentalist view of that process, putting their bets on open information systems and letting the chips fall where they may. But there are nearly 80 million Boomers in America, possessed of deeply felt convictions and boundless confidence, who do not enjoy having their certainties challenged in unmanaged information environments or their positions questioned by those who lack political clout. Quite a few of them occupy positions from which they can influence decisions in great or small ways, and they can withhold their participation if they feel a project threatens their authority.

Technologies such as blogs, wikis, real-time communication systems, and social networks are not just innovative new media for the dissemination of information, but represent a whole new epistemological approach to the way we create consensus reality. It is a profoundly disruptive change to move from a command–and–control management environment where power is predicated on privileged access to information and relationships, to an information space that is radically, genuinely egalitarian, bottom–up, transparent, and self-managed.

Consider blogging. A blogger derives authority exclusively from the quality of the content posted on the blog. Readers credit positions that are well-supported and coherently presented, regardless of the status or credentials of the blogger. Many widely read bloggers are anonymous,[21] or their identities are entirely incidental to their blogging enterprise. Frankness of style—even crudeness—is read to connote authenticity, showing the blogger is not bound by established conventions and therefore represents an independent point of view (independent of corporate PR and government propaganda, in this context). This can be offputting to older readers, particularly Silents who value formality and decorum. Blogs are also participative communities rather than one-way channels of information. Readers can talk back or question the blog owner (or one another) through comments,[22] and enjoy the same privilege of credibility based solely on their qualitative contributions and reputations on the site. Unsurprisingly, according to a 2006 study by the Pew Internet and American Life Project, 54 percent of American bloggers are younger than age 30.[23]

The open, unsupervised quality of blogs can be deeply unsettling to people who have internalized the notion that good information comes only from trusted institutions, credentialed individuals, or valid ideological perspectives. In the last several years, the emergence of insurgent political commentary and literary criticism in the blogosphere has driven some well-established members of the Boomer- and pre-Boomer-dominated media into screaming flights of fury. Critic Richard Schickel (b. 1933)[24] provided one of numerous examples in an editorial published in the *Los Angeles Times* on May 20, 2007:

> Let me put this bluntly, in language even a busy blogger can understand: Criticism—and its humble cousin, reviewing—is not a democratic activity. It is, or should be, an elite enterprise, ideally undertaken by individuals who bring something to the party beyond their hasty, instinctive opinions of a book (or any other cultural object). It is work that requires disciplined taste, historical and theoretical knowledge and a fairly deep sense of the author's (or filmmaker's or painter's) entire body of work, among other qualities.[25]

The decline of standards is the eternal refrain of all older generations, who routinely—and often wrongly—assume that less experienced people are incapable of discerning worthwhile material without the counsel of wise elders. But to Boomers and Silents raised during an era of hierarchical social organization and elite control of discourse, the idea that you could do away with the gatekeeper and still maintain some kind of order and professionalism is preposterous. Boomers know from their own youthful experience that experiments in unbridled freedom can lead to unhappy results, which is why many former radicals have aged into the most stalwart defenders of elites and hierarchies. However, the discomfort of some older critics with the apparent anarchy of grassroots content creation leads them to misjudge the technology, or to strangely suggest that the technology has somehow created threatening critical perspectives that would not otherwise exist.

Despite their openness, collaborative content environments are not free-for-alls. They are self-regulating, substituting the judgment of the community (of readers and commenters) for the standards and biases of an elite editorial board. Blog readers are keenly aware that not all work that appears on blogs is of equal quality or is deserving of equal respect—and they feel far more empowered to voice their feedback to the authors than they would in more formal settings. This can be disconcerting for elites who are accustomed to receiving deference because of their stature, but the transparency generally does more good than harm to the ecology of the information environment as a whole. Bad work is critiqued in the open so mistakes are not repeated; good work and good ideas—even from unlikely sources—gain currency and can spread with unprecedented speed.

Wikis—collaborative information repositories where anyone can contribute or rewrite content—are another potential source of consternation and confusion to people who are accustomed to the institutional validation of truth. Wikipedia, the popular online user-created encyclopedia, is perhaps the most familiar instance of the technology and has hence been the biggest target for criticism.[26] Michael Ross, senior vice president for corporate development of Encyclopedia Britannica, Inc. (not exactly an uninterested party, to be sure), gave voice to the most popular critique in 2004: "How do they know it's accurate? People can put down anything."[27] This is a good question (with a bunch of good answers), but it seems to be more salient to older people than youngsters.[28]

Wikipedia is a special case because it is so public and so popular, but enterprise wikis can elicit the same sort of response. Imagine that a company has deployed a wiki for the sales department, where sales reps enter their observations and experiences after each sales engagement to build a comprehensive profile of each customer. At first, the tool is most popular with younger reps, leading the more experienced salespeople to disregard the value of the content. Eventually, a few of the senior people are persuaded to share some of their tricks of the trade and personal knowledge. They then return to discover that, per the conventions of wiki usage, some of the information they contributed has been edited or augmented by "helpful" junior staffers whose judgment and authority they do not respect. It is not hard to imagine the outcome in an organization that has not set expectations properly or fully embraced the leveling implications of collaborative content creation.

In some cases, the whole concept (or perhaps the name) of a wiki generates unfortunate reactions. James Barrett, a 23-year-old software engineer who blogs at Millennials at Work, reports the following anecdote:

> I am still ridiculed from time to time by coworkers for my support of the wiki concept yet no one can tell me why. InfoWorld.com deemed 2004 as the year of the enterprise wiki, yet it's 2007 and I'm being taunted. It's as if members of older generations are afraid of wikis and other Web 2.0 technologies, like it's a bits and bytes version of the plague. In retrospect I think if I never told anyone that our team site was powered by a wiki engine and just let them have at it, the site would have received a much warmer welcome and it would have achieved my goals of collaboration and distribution of content generation. So I've learned my lesson: in the future when discussing the wiki concept with seasoned members of a large corporate IT department, refer to it as an enterprise grade content management system with lackluster permissions and oversight.[29]

The bottom line is that resistance to collaborative and bottom-up information systems may be rooted in many factors that go beyond the technical complexity and unfamiliarity of the technology. These factors can be overcome, so long as organizations recognize and address the underlying cultural and generational people problems.

WHY IT MATTERS: CAPTURING KNOWLEDGE

The single greatest organizational challenge related to the aging workforce around the world is the retention of knowledge. Older workers have built up lifetimes of experience, insights, and relationships that enhance the performance of their organizations in ways great and small. This knowledge constitutes a source of capital every bit as valuable as physical or financial assets. When it is lost, it can often be relearned only at great cost. Some useful things older workers might know include:

- Where to obtain parts for the out-of-production machine tool, and how to fix it when it goes down
- The names, birthdays, and favorite colors of the grandchildren of the firm's biggest client
- The information that was left out of the manual, that you'd only figure out after screwing up a couple of times and wondering what you were doing wrong
- The precedents that an agency has recognized for granting exceptions to a documented policy
- The *real* arrangement with the people who supply towels and soap in the washroom

These are somewhat whimsical examples, but they have real-life consequences every time a valued older employee retires from an organization. David DeLong, in *Lost Knowledge* (2004), identifies five principal risks associated with knowledge loss:

- Ability to innovate is reduced.
- Ability to pursue growth strategies is threatened.
- Reduced efficiency undermines low-cost strategy.

- Losing knowledge can give competitors an advantage.
- Losing specific knowledge at the wrong time increases vulnerability.[30]

Knowledge management (KM) initiatives have been underway in organizations since the 1980s. Typically they involved systematically documenting informal or tacit knowledge, creating mentor–pupil relationships for the person-to-person transfer of knowledge and relationships, and building reusable repositories of practices and processes that could integrate organizational knowledge into day-to-day tasks. The increasing capabilities of IT systems made them a natural match for these KM efforts, at least in theory. Popular KM solutions enabled people to contribute to searchable databases so that others in the organization could access their experience and insights instantly, over the network. Distance learning via videoconference also promised to reduce the costs and friction associated with person-to-person contact so that rich, interactive information transfers could occur in informal, real-time settings without the overhead costs of getting people together in the same physical space.

In practice, many first-generation KM systems failed to deliver on this promise for several reasons that have nothing to do with technology, including low management commitment, user trust issues ("what is the company going to do with me once my knowledge is in the system?"), poor incentives for users who contributed, and poor quality of contributed content. However, it didn't help that the software programs supporting KM activities were difficult to use and poorly integrated with the normal routines of work.

Today, Web 2.0 technologies provide an alternative to the old centralized, top-down approaches to KM. Blogs, wikis, social networks, podcasts, voice and video over IP, semantic search, reputation systems, and collaborative workspaces give people easier, more natural ways to participate in organic communities of knowledge. The unstructured give-and-take of these less formal environments encourages people to contribute in their own voice and style. Information is recognizable as human insight, rather than being the impersonal output of a knowledge system. This makes it easier to build trust and social capital within the knowledge community and gives people better ways to contextualize the information they get out of the system. With the integration of presence awareness and real-time communication technology into the social networking application environment, it is possible for people to start spontaneous conversations around content in the system, laying the basis for authentic relationships that lead to deep, durable knowledge transfer.

Technological innovation does not solve the preexisting management challenges around KM, but it does make the implementation of solutions potentially less painful for users once the other necessary components of a KM strategy are in place. Participating in organic communities and real conversations is more compelling than interacting with a database or sorting through a videotape library; recording a podcast or updating a blog is less intrusive than filling out a project report or entering data into a structured system.

The generational problem with KM systems is that they are usually asymmetrical with respect to age. Younger people have greater facility with the technology and are relatively more open to making the changes to their workstyle that collaborative systems require, but older users have the perishable experience and knowledge that needs to be captured. Web 2.0 technologies that appear easy and accessible to 30- and 40-something IT planners may pose fundamental usability problems for older users, even in organizations that provide strong management backing and cultural support to knowledge-sharing efforts. More significantly, the most compelling benefits of collaborative knowledge systems—integration, informality, democratized access to communication channels, distributed decision making—are most likely to activate pockets of generational resistance because of the disruptions they cause to traditional patterns of authority.

OUTLOOK

The success of Web 2.0 technologies in KM therefore depends on making sure that older knowledge contributors are comfortable with both the technical and cultural implications, by offering clear, age-appropriate technology training and addressing hidden generational concerns directly. Some specific practices are discussed in Chapter 9. Addressing the issues of knowledge management in the full context of generational differences in workstyle and technology adoption can help increase the success of KM initiatives, reduce the risks associated with knowledge loss, and surmount the unique but often hidden barriers facing older workers.

ENDNOTES

1. "Boomers: The Next 20 Years." The Institute for the Future, 2006. www.iftf.org/docs/IFTF_Boomers.pdf

2. Tulgan, Bruce. "The Continuing Generational Shift in the Workforce." RainMakerThinking Inc. March 21, 2005. www. rainmaker thinking.com/backwttw/2005/mar15.htm

3. Excerpts taken from Jobing.com online article "What's Next? Most Boomers Aren't Ready for a Permanent Vacation." *Wall Street Journal*, December 20, 2004.

4. U.S Census Bureau. July 2006. http://www.census.gov/Press-Release/www/releases/archives/facts_for_features_special_editions/007125.html

5. Strauss, William, and Neil Howe. *Generations: A History of America's Future, 1584–2069*. New York: Vintage, 1991, pp. 279–294.

6. Zemke, Ron, Claire Raines, and Bob Filipczak. *Generations at Work: Managing the Clash of Veterans, Boomers, Xers and Nexters in Your Workplace*. AMACOM/American Management Association, 2000, p. 79.

7. Todaro, Wendy. "Want to Be a CEO? Stay Put." March 31, 2003. www.forbes.com/2003/03/31/cx_wt_0401exec.html

8. Lancaster, Lynne, and David Stillman. *When Generations Collide: Who They Are, Why They Clash. How to Solve the Generational Puzzle at Work.* Collins Business, 2002, p. 127.

9. "So-called Retirement." So Baby Boomer: Life Tips Blog, September 22, 2006

10. *Wall Street Journal,* December 16, 2006, and UBS Research Focus. "Demographics: A Coming of Age." Wealth Management Research, April 2006. www.ubs.com/wmresearch

11. "Boomer Survey: We'll Have to Work During Retirement." Thrivent Financial for Lutherans, December 7, 2006. www.news max.com/money/archives/articles/2006/11/15/093811.cfm

12. American Association of Retired Persons (AARP).

13. Gardner, Marilyn. "Age Friendly Workplaces on the Rise." *The Christian Science Monitor,* May 7, 2007. http://www.csmonitor.com/2007/0507/p13s02-wmgn.html

14. "Demographic Profile: American Baby Boomers." Metlife Mature Market Institute Analysis, 2000. http://www.metlife.com/WPSAssets/34442486101113318029V1FBoomer%20Profile%202005.pdf

15. McPherson, Doug. "Employers See 50+ Workers as Golden Asset." *The Denver Post,* January 28, 2007.

16. Reimer, Jeremy. "Total Share: 30 Years of Personal Computer Market Share Figures." December 14, 2005. http://arstechnica.com/articles/culture/total-share.ars/1

17. News Release Society for Industrial and Organizational Psychology. March 10, 2005. http://www.agingworkforcenews.com/2005_03_01_archive.html

18. Pew Internet & American Life Project.

19. *Generations at Work,* p. 79.

20. Daffner, Beverly. Interview with the author. June 2, 2007.

21. Approximately 55 percent of all bloggers are anonymous, according to the Pew Internet and American Life Project (Lenhart, Amanda, and Susannah Fox, *Bloggers: A Portrait of the Internet's New Storytellers,* July 2006, p. 2).

22. Nine out of ten blogs allow or encourage comments. (*Ibid,* Lenhart and Fox, p. 4.)

23. *Ibid,* p. 2.

24. According to his Wikipedia entry.

25. Schickel, Richard. "Not Everyone's a Critic." *The Los Angeles Times*, May 20, 2007. http://www.latimes.com/news/opinion/la-op-schickel20may20,0,7430993.story?coll=la-opinion-rightrail

26. Ironically, the best overview of the various criticisms of Wikipedia, which span everything from quality of information to charges of bias to technologist Jaron Lanier's claim that "the hive mind is for the most part boring and stupid," is Wikipedia itself, http://en.wikipedia.org/wiki/Wikipedia:Criticisms

27. Quoted in Bray, H. "A Great Source—If You Can Trust It." *The Boston Globe*, July 12, 2004.

28. Perhaps the recent development of a tool that can track the IP addresses of Wikipedia contributors may add some confidence to the process.

29. Barrett, James. "Wiki Woes." Millennials at Work Blog, posted August 3, 2007. http://millennialsatwork.wordpress.com/2007/08/03/wiki-woes/

30. DeLong, David. *Lost Knowledge.* New York: Oxford Press, 2004, p. 31.

~ 5 ~

Younger Workers: With Great Potential Comes Great Expectations

At the opposite end of the spectrum from the aging Boomers are the new kids on the block: the Millennials. Pundits started tracking the Class of 2000 when they were in kindergarten, reading the tea leaves of rising test scores and a distinctly different attitude toward parents, school, and society than their GenX elders. Early reports on the abilities and attitudes of Millennials are largely positive, if sometimes tinged with caveats about their sense of entitlement. The word on Millennials: they're good, they're numerous, they're the future, and they know it.

Issues of technology policy have followed Millennials through life, from debates over violent video games and inappropriate Web content to controversies about illegal music downloading, teen cell phone use, and the meteoric rise of social networking sites. These issues will follow them into the workplace as well. As the Millennials arrive, their productivity and motivation will hinge on the ability of their employers to adapt, both culturally and technologically, to their unique workstyles.

Millennials come armed with expectations as high as their potential. Networked digital natives don't merely want high-tech tools as status symbols or playthings: they rely on them to fill gaps in knowledge and experience, and to enable a workstyle that depends on massive levels of multitasking and rapid-fire access to new information. Some experts claim these tools are the basis of their cognitive approach to the way they solve problems, communicate and collaborate with one another, find and share information, and express themselves creatively. The ability to use the Internet, sophisticated collaboration environments, media, communication, and mobile devices is central to achieving the integration between work and life that is the overwhelming priority and motivator of younger workers. Millennials are aware of this and often have more thoughtful and informed opinions on the subject than many of their elders. Boomers and GenXers may also be surprised at how the generational values and worldview of the Millennials influence the way they view technology's transformative potential.

Organizations with an older center of gravity to their workforce or a conservative approach to their IT architecture may feel they can ignore these issues, or segregate bleeding-edge technology to more youthful workgroups and divisions. As workforce transition accelerates over the next 10 to 15 years, that approach will become increasingly unsustainable, and IT departments will either need to provide the complex and collaborative knowledge environments younger workers need or face making themselves, and possibly their organizations, irrelevant.

WHO ARE THE MILLENNIALS?

The Millennials, also known as Generation Y (or Why), NetGen (Tapscott's preferred term), the Digital Generation, Echo Boomers, and a handful of other clever nicknames, are the colorful children of the end of the 20th century, born after 1980 (the year birthrates in the United States began to match pre-1963 levels) and now entering young adulthood. The early verdict on the Millennials was pronounced by Strauss and Howe in *Millennials Rising* (2000): they are optimistic, moral, socially aware, globally conscious, collaborative, and bright—a generation of achievers with the potential for heroism.[1] Their generational personality is that of civic institution builders—a profile last seen among the Veterans of World War II. Is it any wonder that they are the subject of such avid interest in the job market and in society at large?

Millennials have only recently arrived in the workforce in significant numbers. The oldest of them are just hitting their mid-twenties, and only the most precocious have established themselves in their fields and careers. Their very first graduates of professional schools arrived in law firms, accountancies, and management trainee programs in 2006 and 2007. The first Millennial doctors will begin their residencies in 2008, and the first of this generation's PhDs will start gaining tenure on university faculties in the early 2010s. Those who served in the armed forces out of high school or college will have had the most intensive combat experience of any Americans since Vietnam.

So far, the most visible members of this generation in the media are those whose talents or family backgrounds qualify them for celebrity in sports and entertainment, such as actors Elijah Wood and Scarlett Johansson, Indy driver Danica Patrick, basketball star LeBron James, and assorted pop musicians like Kelly Clarkson and Kanye West. So far, the most visible under-25 entrepreneurs are the founders of the social networking site Facebook (Mark Zuckerberg, Andrew McCallum, Dustin Moskovitz, and Chris Hughes), while political writers Matthew Yglesias and Ezra Klein parlayed their well-respected blogs[2] into burgeoning careers as mainstream media pundits when both were barely out of college. Other Millennials have become minor celebrities through the use of YouTube, MySpace, and other 21st-century media.

By the numbers, there are approximately 80 million Millennials in the United States[3]—greater in absolute numbers than the Boomers, and a veritable tidal wave of youth compared with the 51 million Generation Xers that preceded them. They are less white and less English-speaking than any previous generation: one in three American Millennials is non-Caucasian. About 50 percent are from single-parent families, and 80 percent come from families where the mother worked outside the home.

Throughout their lives, most Millennials have been welcomed and celebrated by their parents (often late-breeding Boomers), who filled their lives with scheduled activities, moral instruction, and nurturing attention designed to spur the development of their character and intellect and prepare them for success in a competitive world. Education since the mid-1980s has focused on diversity, teamwork, self-esteem, and most of all, success. "This generation has been more strategically educated than any other generation," said Mike Sciola, the Director of the Career Resource Center at Wesleyan University.[4] While many Millennials have been criticized for gaps in their knowledge, particularly of history and social studies, they often emerge from their educational experience with a spirit of can-do optimism not seen in America since the halcyon days of the Boomers in the early 1960s.

According to a Pew Research Poll published in January 2007, Millennials are a happy bunch: 93 percent are "very happy" or "pretty happy" with various aspects of their lives, including family relationships, job satisfaction, finances, and the amount of free time they have; 74 percent rate their life expectations for the next five years as "highest/best"; and 68 percent agree that they constitute a unique generation.[5]

As teenagers and young adults, they are better-behaved than their elders were at the same stage of life. Drug use, teen pregnancy, suicide, and violent crime have all declined as the Millennials have come of age, while average scores on standardized tests have inched up. Rates of drinking among college freshmen in 2005 were lower than any year since 1966.[6] According to Monitoring the Future, a highly regarded annual survey, cigarette and alcohol consumption in grades 8, 10, and 12 are now at their lowest levels since the survey began in 1975.[7]

Millennials are ambitious: 87 percent of those in high school say they hope to attend college,[8] and 64 percent of Millennials in the Pew Survey said that the number-one goal of their generation was to "get rich" (51 percent say getting famous is the first or second goal, compared to 30 percent who responded "to help people in need"). And they expect to achieve their financial goals: 74 percent of the students expect to be better off than their parents in terms of income and quality of life over their lifetime, and 65 percent of college students surveyed by Ernst & Young (Canada) in 2001 expected to be millionaires by the age of 30.[9]

They are entrepreneurial: Bureau of Labor Statistics data for 2005 show that some 370,000 young people ages 16 to 24 were self-employed, the occupational category that includes entrepreneurs. "People are realizing they don't have to go to work in suits and ties and don't have to talk about budgets every day," says Ben Kaufman, a 20-year-old entrepreneur quoted in a recent piece in *USA Today*. "They can have a job they like. They can create a job for themselves."[10]

"There's such a frontier for possible business ideas," says Scott Neuberger, 25, CEO of Boston-based Collegeboxes. "The barrier to entry is very low and doesn't require a lot of money in a lot of cases. I think there's more of an entrepreneurial spirit in our generation than perhaps in other generations. Being an entrepreneur has become cool and sexy."[11]

"The new American Dream is much more entrepreneurial," says Anya Kamenetz, blogger and author of the book *Generation Debt*. "And it's about shaping one's own destiny: mobility, flexibility to do your own work and the ability to have a career as an expression of who you are as a person."[12]

And they are community-oriented. Volunteerism is the standard among this cohort: 69 percent overall volunteered for community service in the past year, with high school students at 77 percent, according to a 2006 Harvard study.[13] Social entrepreneurship classes at colleges and universities are oversubscribed. Political participation among youth is at a 20-year high.

Heidi Locke Simon, a partner in the San Francisco office of management consulting firm Bain & Co., quoted in *Business Week* (May 2005), summed up the Millennial work ethic this way: "Instead of a simple 100-hour week, now the model is: work 60 hours a week, devote 20 hours to nonprofit, and spend 20 hours writing a plan to start your own business."[14]

MILLENNIALS AND TECHNOLOGY

There's one label that all observers of the Millennial generation agree on: tech-savvy. Technology plays a central role in the lives of Millennials. It has surrounded and pervaded their lives since birth, constantly evolving into a higher state of connectedness, vividness, and interactivity.

Carolyn Miller and Bruce Tulgin write in *Managing Generation Y* (2001):

> Tech-savvy [Millennials] are now usurping "intellectual authority" in their homes and classrooms, leaving parents and teachers both confused and awed. They can access a world of information and master increasingly complex systems faster than their elders. They're consultants to parents and collaborators with teachers, infusing technology into the curriculum. They're proud owners of impressive electronic portfolios filled with website designs, home pages and Internet resource guides. They know how to use the Internet as efficiently as older generations used the library, but in this case, gaining *instant* access to people, events and ideas.[15]

Technology Is Everywhere

The life span of the Millennials tracks closely with the spread of PCs and communication technology in the United States and around the world. In 1981, the first birth year of the Millennial cohort, computers were expensive novelties: only 600,000 PCs were sold in the United States.[16] By the end of the year 2000, they were ubiquitous, with nearly 169 million computers in use in homes and businesses around the country.[17] Starting in the early 1990s, mobile telephones began their upward growth curve. In the mid-1990s, Internet access took off. By the middle of the 2000s, broadband connectivity was pushing upward to 50 percent.

Figures 5.1 through 5.4 chart the growth of personal computers, Internet usage, mobile phone usage, and broadband connectivity in the United States over the 25-year life span of this generation.

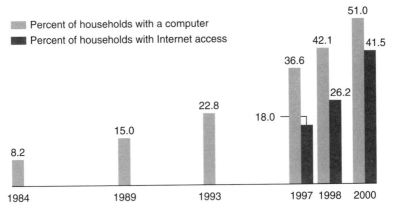

Note: Data on Internet access were not collected before 1997.
Source: U.S. Census Bureau, Current Population Survey, various years.

FIGURE 5.1 Computers and Internet Access in the Home: 1984 to 2000 (Civilian noninstitutional population)

Source: Reimer, Jeremy. "Total share: 30 years of personal computer market share figures." December 14, 2005. http://arstechnica.com/articles/culture/total-share.ars/1.

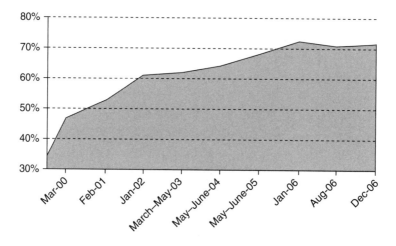

FIGURE 5.2 Percentage of U.S. Adults Online

Source: Pew Internet & American Life Project Surveys, March 2000–December 2006.

The 2007 study by the Pew Research Center for People and the Press also polled on technology issues. They found that 86 percent of Millennials surveyed report they use the Internet occasionally (compared with 91 percent of

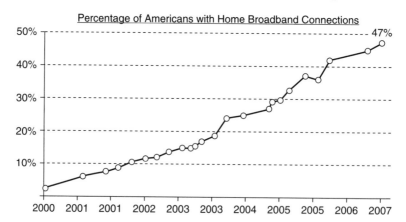

FIGURE 5.3 Percent of Americans with Home Broadband Connections, 2000–2007

Source: Horrigan, John B. "Why It Will Be Hard to Close the Broadband Divide." Pew Internet & American Life Project, August 1, 2007. http://pewresearch.org/pubs/556/why-it-will-be-hard-to-close-the-broadband-divide.

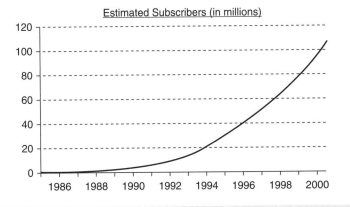

FIGURE 5.4 Estimated Cell Subscribers, 1986–2000*

Source: Gaudin, Sharon. "Cell phone facts and statistics." Network World, July 2, 2001. http://www.networkworld.com/research/2001/0702featside.html.

GenXers, 76 percent of Boomers, and 46 percent of Seniors). More than half use real-time communications technology such as instant messaging or texting—about double the rate of GenXers, four times that of Boomers, and over ten times that of seniors. Nearly seven Millennials in ten think technology is a "good way to make friends"—far and away the highest of any generational group surveyed.[18]

Researchers Reynol Junco and Jeanna Mastrodicasa found that in a survey of 7,705 U.S. college students conducted during the spring and fall semesters of 2006:

- 75.5 percent use some type of instant messaging program, with 15 percent logged on 24 hours a day, 7 days a week.

- 91.9 percent multitask (perform several tasks simultaneously that require cognitive resources and attention).

- 27.9 percent report having blogs, compared to 7 percent of all adults.

- Nearly half have downloaded music over peer-to-peer networks, and 20.3 percent have downloaded movies (that number has undoubtedly risen since the survey was taken).

- 68.5 percent reported having accounts with the Facebook social network, and log in twice a day.[19]

Digital Natives

For Millennials, information technology is not a threat, not a novelty, not even a tool. It just *is*. Asking them about it is like asking a fish about water. At a very early point in their development, most Millennials intuited the underlying logic of information technology the same way they acquired the grammar of their native language. It's not just that they know how to use specific features of programs and devices: when presented with an unfamiliar piece of technology, they understand the approaches necessary to unlock its secrets because they understand the way it *should* work.

"We are a generation of learners by exploration," writes Millennial Carrie Windham of her early experience with technology. "My first Web site, for example, was constructed before I had any concept of HTML or Java. I simply experimented with the commands until the pieces fit together."[20]

Educator Mark Prensky, in his influential 2001 essay "Digital Natives, Digital Immigrants," suggests that kids raised in the era of digital technology have experienced a profound and fundamental change in their thinking patterns and possibly even their brain chemistry. "Digital Natives are used to receiving information really fast," Prensky writes. "They like to parallel process and multi-task. They prefer their graphics before their text rather than the opposite. They prefer random access (like hypertext). They function best when networked. They thrive on instant gratification and frequent rewards. They prefer games to 'serious' work."[21]

These habits were reinforced throughout the adolescence of many Millennials by extremely complex video games and interactive activities on the Internet. About 49 percent of Millennials polled by Pew play video games, compared to 35 percent of Generation Xers and minuscule percentages of older adults.[22] Game designers, most of whom are young people, consciously created streamlined processes to rapidly teach players gameplay methods and game objectives, understanding that most of their audience would learn by doing rather than reading a manual. In the competitive context of gaming, young people had great incentive to acquire complex and arcane skills quickly, through intuition as well as trial-and-error. Gamers learned to win by thinking along with the game developers, thereby incidentally internalizing the work habits and creative sensibilities of professional software programmers. It is little wonder that many are almost instantly adept at the comparatively simple tasks of multimedia authoring, design, and information architecture. It also has interesting implications when a generation raised on video games begins exerting influence on management decisions, as we will see in Chapter 6.

That said, not every Millennial is a technophile. Millennials are at least as sophisticated in their views of technology as any other age group. They recognize—better than many—the potential and manifest dangers of technology. Some are impatient with the relentless complexity and critical of the way some of their peers use mediated communication as a substitute for personal connection, conversation, and engagement. According to Pew, strong majorities of young people believe technology makes people lazier (74 percent), makes people more isolated (65 percent), and causes people to waste time (68 percent).[23] "Even though they're with their peers, they're wrapped up in electronic conversations, and they lose track of body language and those signals that are around to what's happening," says Linda Walter, who runs family-orientation sessions for freshmen at Seton Hall University in South Orange, New Jersey.[24]

Because they are so familiar with technology, Millennials have remarkably deep, well-informed opinions on its transformative possibilities and social implications that can be of great help to forward-looking organizations, as we will see in Chapter 8. They are conscious of the way their technology proficiency separates them from their elders and can be sensitive to the implications of that gap in a social or workplace context.

Unlike crusading Boomers and efficiency-demanding GenXers, most Millennials are not evangelists or teachers by nature. They use technology as the foundation for their collaborative and institution-building projects but neither expect nor care if others participate with them. Organizations that want their younger workers to act as coaches or guides in the technology area will need to make those expectations explicit and furnish specific training to acculturate them to the different learning styles of older adults.

MILLENNIALS IN THE WORKFORCE

The generational personality of Millennials and their close relationship with technology has several implications for their future as participants in the workforce. Some of these implications will be disruptive, even painful, for organizations that are accustomed to traditional patterns of authority and channels of communication. Some will seem ridiculously indulgent, reflecting a deference to youth that middle-aged decision makers never received when they were getting started on the lower rungs of their career ladders. And some will entail risky, forward-leaning investments in technology that IT departments may not be prepared to make.

Millennials, by and large, will not wait around while potential employers equivocate. They are ready and willing to quit, move back in with their parents ("boomerang"), return to school, start their own businesses, or offer their talents to competitors. Neil Howe, co-author of *Millennials Rising: The Next Great Generation*, says that moving back in with parents is a way to avoid wasting a lot of time. According to Howe, when it comes to careers, "Boomerangers want to get it right the first time. If you don't have to worry about paying rent, you have more flexibility to wait for the right job and to take a job that feels very right but pays very poorly." The widespread acceptance of boomeranging as a life strategy for young adults makes the economic factors of employment less important than the value of the opportunity, and allows talented Millennials to take advantage of low-paid or unpaid internships to get a jump start on career development.[25]

Even progressive workplaces will have trouble retaining younger workers if they can't offer sufficient challenge and opportunity on an ongoing basis. This is not to say that young people will quit because of inadequate technology in and of itself, but they may perceive inadequate technology as an indicator of an organizational culture that does not offer them the general kind of opportunities they are looking for. Dychtwald, Erickson, and Morison sum up the problem as follows:

> Given their independence and libertarian leanings, [younger workers] expect to be treated individually, they want flexible schedules, they know their careers belong to them (not their employers), and so they value knowledge and skill more than tenure. Given their ambition, they want to contribute quickly, not work in the background. Given their technology proficiency, they appreciate up-to-date technology in the workplace, and they expect to manage their own information and communication. . . . They want to be heard on the job, they want frequent and useful feedback, and they expect to make their work fit in with other

life commitments and pursuits. Since they tend to be tribal and socially-networked, they want sociable workplaces, they want to connect with others (including mentors).[26]

Millennial Characteristics

The table below summarizes the culture and technology implications of Millennial generational characteristics.

Millennial Characteristic	Culture Implication	Technology Implication
Inquisitive	Greater transparency, greater willingness by management to explain decisions	Systems that provide visible metrics and relationships, reputation tracking, etc.
Social	Flatter, more networked organization	Social networks and contact management tools
Ambitious/ Impatient	Immediate feedback	Real-time communication
Global Orientation	Commitment to diversity	Open communication and information channels
Respectful of Authority	Mentoring programs	Social networks and expertise location systems

Inquisitive   Millennials want to know why. Books and articles offering management advice to would-be employers are peppered with warnings about providing strategic context to young workers, even those starting out in low-level operational roles. "They're ambitious, they're demanding and they question everything, so if there isn't a good reason for that long commute or late night, don't expect them to do it," warns a May, 2007 profile of the new twentysomething generation in *Fortune* magazine.[27]

Technology provides organizations with ways to enable the kind of transparency that Millennials demand. Intranets can post mission statements and org charts, but that's not all. Real-time performance data from enterprise systems can provide front-line workers with insights into how their efforts contribute to overall team and organizational goals. Reputation systems that allow readers to rank the relevance of content, the quality of service, or other performance metrics can give Millennials the instant feedback they crave and the context to better understand management decisions affecting their work. Really Simple Syndication (RSS) feeds and subscription-based multimedia services such as podcasts can push information into the hands of interested parties to provide a continuously updated frame of reference for individual and group activities, as well as timely knowledge of new practices. It may not be clear to today's IT managers why these sorts of capabilities should be integrated into the work environment of people whose roles do not require them. However, as the inquisitive culture of the Millennials begins to pervade organizations, the value of self-service tools for transparency will become obvious.

Social According to David Stillman, co-author of *When Generations Collide*, Millennials have "the group-think mentality. When you are raised to collaborate at home, then you are taught how to do that in middle school and practice it in college, you show up at work saying 'Where's my team?' They're just comfortable working with peers."[28] Millennials have worked together on the playground, in the classroom, around the world, and in their busy social lives. This teamwork is facilitated by an ever-expanding constellation of technologies that allow for self-expression (blogs and personal pages on social networking sites), not-always-legal sharing of content (peer-to-peer networks like LimeWire and tools like Bit-Torrent), instant person-to-person contact (instant messaging, texting, video chatting), and communal activities around shared interests (fan Web sites).

Millennials bring a more open approach to collaboration than many managers and IT departments today might be comfortable with. Approximately 54 percent of 18- to 25-year-olds surveyed by Pew reported using social networking sites; 77 percent of Millennials believe that they share "too much" personal information on such sites. According to a Clearswift Poll in 2007, 63 percent of office workers access social networking sites at least once per day, 51 percent report spending at least one hour per week on such sites, and *46 percent discuss work-related issues on social networking sites*.[29] The numbers are even more dramatic among today's teens.[30] According to a Harrison poll, 68 percent of teens have personal sites on social networks, and 25 percent keep in contact daily.[31]

Ambitious—Impatient/Entitled Like young people of all generations, Millennials want what they want and they want it *now!* But unlike their elders, they have gotten used to receiving it—from parents, society, and technology. To Millennials accustomed to the immediate feedback of real-time technology like video games, IM, and texting, even e-mail can seem glacially slow.

Millennials "have high expectations of technology, and when it doesn't measure up, they get impatient," write Martin and Tulgan.[32] This doesn't just mean they expect managers to answer their e-mails in seconds. If their employers are not broadly and quickly responsive to their technology needs, young workers may well take matters into their own hands by using solutions that fall outside IT governance or start looking elsewhere for situations that better suit their skills and workstyle.

Impatience doesn't end with technology. Millennials are far more apt to leave jobs that do not meet their personal goals or fit their life plan. The traditional economic leverage enjoyed by employers only goes so far with this generation, 72 percent of whom believe they will find another good-paying job relatively quickly and easily.[33] An article appearing in the June 7, 2007 *Wall Street Journal* relates the following anecdote:

Ryan Paugh, 23, is already concerned that he's wasting his life at his first full-time job. In January, the Flemington, N.J., resident started working as a contractor, with no benefits, in the communications department of a Fortune 500 company. Frequently, he finishes a day's work in three hours, he says. "You feel really useless." Up until recently, Mr. Paugh asked for more work from his boss every other day. "Once in a while they hand something off," he says. Now he doesn't ask so much. "Maybe you're just paying your dues, but how do you know you're not just sitting around, waiting to get fired?" he wonders. Mr. Paugh says the situation is making him depressed.

"I think it has a lot to do with the high expectations we were brought up with. 'You can do it. You can have what you want,'" Lindahl says. "We're criticized for wanting it all: high pay, purposeful work, flexible hours. It's hard for people in our generation just to do work."[34]

"There are many reasons for high turnover," writes author and blogger Penelope Trunk, "but the most fundamental one is that Boomers have set up a work place that uses financial bribes to get people to give up their time: Work sixty hours a week and we'll pay you six figures. [Millennials] will not have this. To hold out money as a carrot is insulting to a generation raised to think personal development is the holy grail of time spent well."[35]

"They were told, 'You're smart, you're different, you're the smartest generation, you're the most tech-savvy, you're going to be different. It's about finding out, you know, who you are, and fulfilling that,'" says Jane Buckingham, President of The Intelligence Group, a marketing firm that studies generational trends. "It's a great message, but not when you then have to go fit into a mold in a company."[36]

Global Orientation "[The] Millennials' world is far more expansive than previous generations' because, through on-line social networks, they can reach well beyond the confines of geography and establish relationships with others. They're ideally positioned to support our global workplaces, and HR people should tap their skills accordingly," observes

Jeanne Achille, CEO of The Devon Group, in a May 2007 article in *HR Magazine*.[37] The experience of making personal connections on a global scale has shaped the outlook of Millennials in many ways. They are more open to diversity, more likely to consider the global implications of their personal actions, and more engaged in issues such as environmental policy and corporate citizenship.

This global network is a unique asset that many Millennials use to gain information, outside perspective, and helpful contacts, but maintaining it takes time. Instant Messaging (IM) is the communication medium of choice, with its immediate feedback, low cost, and ability to see at a glance who is available for social conversation. "I use IM to communicate with friends in different cities, countries, rooms, etc. I mainly use it to stay in touch with people, especially those I wouldn't normally call since it's easier and less awkward to simply send a message over IM," said Cherie Wilson, a graduate student in political economy and a participant in Microsoft's Board of the Future program in 2005.

Respect for Authority   In a study conducted by two researchers from Emory University's Goizueta Business School, nearly 70 percent of Millennials agreed with the statement that "Authority figures should set and enforce rules," compared to around 40 percent of GenXers. About 60 percent of Millennials agreed with the statement "I trust authority figures to act in my best interest," whereas only 40 percent of GenXers agreed.[38]

It's a curious paradox that the generation that questions everything is nevertheless more respectful of individuals and institutions that have earned their trust. So far, though, the track record shows that Millennials get along better with their parents, teachers, and much older coworkers than either Boomers or GenXers. They are also well-regarded by their elders, especially in the area of technological prowess.

For this reason, many experts suggest that mentoring programs may be an especially effective way of integrating Millennials into the culture of organizations and bringing them up to speed on the formal and informal knowledge they need to be effective. Mentoring programs can be face-to-face or mediated by technology. The consulting firm KPMG is a recognized leader in this area, with an extensive mentoring program supported by a Web site to facilitate knowledge transfer and informal activities.[39] Older Adults Technology Services (OATS), discussed in Chapter 7, has built an intergenerational program where tech-savvy youth tutor older adults on computer skills while gaining valuable life-skills insights through an unusually mutually respectful relationship with an older mentor.

Millennial Priorities

The table below summarizes the implications of Millenial priorities.

Millennial Priorities	Culture Implication	Technology Implication
Work/Life Balance	Greater integration between work and life at the workplace	Remote access and mobility, access to personal networks at work
Making a Difference	Greater worker participation in policies	Two-way channels of internal communication
Developing Portable Skills	Reduce specialization around process, reemphasis on deep competencies	Training and mentoring programs; standard, accessible technologies
Gaining Approval and Recognition	More hands-on management	Blogs and other channels for personal expression

Work/Life—Balance or Integration?   Millennials were heavily scheduled as kids and learned to balance multiple commitments and activities as part of their way of functioning in the world. Consequently, data consistently shows that balance and flexibility are critical priorities for Millennials entering the workforce, as they were for Generation X previously. For example, 50 percent of Millennial college students surveyed in 2001 say having flexibility in planning a career around major life events is the most important element for achieving a good balance between a career and personal life.[40]

When older cohorts talk about work/life balance, the issues are more about finding time to take care of kids or aging parents, to spend time in personal relationships, or to pursue interests outside of work. The goal is to gain *separation* between work and life to make more room for the latter. Millennials, most of whom don't have kids or dependent elderly parents yet, may see it somewhat differently. James Barrett, the 20-something author of the blog Millennials at Work, puts it this way:

> My opinion is that those members of the Millennial Generation are not interested in the same work-life balance that their older coworkers are interested in. Those more seasoned generations are interested in a more harsh separation between work life and personal life. They prefer to leave work at work and check their personal lives at the company's front door. I see younger workers less interested in a harsh separation and actually prefer to integrate personal and work into one entity, I guess we could just call that 'life'. I want to be able to work from wherever, whenever. The thought is that work is something that you do, not a place that you go. I want to take personal phone calls while I'm at work, access my personal email, and better yet, access to members of my personal life.[41]

Many organizations have only recently come to grips with flextime, telework, sabbaticals, and other work/life balance programs to meet the needs of burned-out Boomers and newly nesting GenXers. From a technology standpoint, those programs can be facilitated through high-speed networks, remote access, and mobile devices to allow people to stay connected away from the office. Work/life *integration* adds another dimension—not just the ability to do work from a life setting (e.g., at home or while doing life and family-oriented activities), but the ability to participate in life from a work setting.

What do organizations say to otherwise-productive young employees who don't recognize boundaries, or the need for boundaries, between doing project-oriented work and chatting with social contacts on IM or playing games online during the workday? "I don't pay you to sit around here and hang out in SecondLife all day!" exclaims the angry manager. A Millennial employee might well reply, "Yes, but you're paying me to do X, Y, and Z, and I'm doing all of those things a lot faster and better than people who spend all day on them, and besides, I've been getting some good advice on dealing with a customer problem from one of my buddies in here." Welcome to the world of work/life balance, Millennial style.

Making a Difference   According to a 2006 national study of 1,800 Millennials by two strategic marketing firms, 79 percent of respondents said they wanted to work for a company that "cares about how it impacts society," and 68 percent would refuse to work at a company that is not socially responsible.[42] This tracks with numerous other studies and observations showing that Millennials are engaged and concerned about social issues, including the environment, labor standards, globalization, diversity, and corporate citizenship. They recognize the role of the individual in contributing to the solution to these problems and will hold their employers to high standards in terms of being consistent with their stated ideals.

If this sounds like an echo of the early Boomers, who stormed into the workforce in the late 1960s demanding reforms and new standards, that's only half right. Boomers are attracted to ideas and give credit to organizations with strongly stated values and missions; Millennials are more results-oriented in their social views. They'd rather *do* than talk. When assessing the suitability of a potential employer, Millennials will be motivated more by the actual performance of the organization and the opportunities it affords for positive results than by its reputation or claims made by its PR department. And once employed, they will judge the company based on their experiences and observations, with unprecedented outlets for making their judgments known to their peers and the public. "With one click of the mouse, they can tell thousands of other people, 'Don't go to work for XYZ company,'" says Barbara Dwyer, CEO of The Job Journey, a soft-skills training firm for high school and community college students in El Macero, California. "It's going to be challenging."[43] Wal-Mart discovered the dual-edged quality of social networking sites in the summer of 2007, when students took advantage of its Facebook site to post negative comments about the company's business practices.[44]

Millennials are much more aware of the global implications of their work, not just because the workplace and the world are so much more connected and transparent as a result of ubiquitous information networks, but because it is part of their generational culture to see themselves as connected to larger processes. Unlike GenXers, who rationalize even odious jobs as an economic necessity, or Boomers, who can rationalize practically anything and affirm it as a positive value, Millennials want their work to directly reflect their personal ethics. The requirement for skilled younger workers may therefore exert some real pressure on organizations to change the way they operate. As Nobel Prize–winning economist and former World Bank official Joseph Stiglitz suggests, socially responsible companies "may benefit from the higher quality labor force that they attract and improved morale: their workers feel better about working for a company that is socially responsible."[45]

From a technology standpoint, organizations can accommodate the values of younger workers by making socially conscious workplace practices more participative, responsive, and transparent. Internal blogs and message boards provide informal two-way communication channels that give workers opportunities to express their views on larger company policies. As importantly, these communication channels can give leadership a window into the real state of worker attitudes and morale, which can be critical factors in the success or failure of their larger goals.

Oliver Young, an analyst for Forrester Research, describes a conversation he had with the CEO of a large, traditional insurance company that was experimenting with social networks and distributed decision-making tools:[46]

> I asked him, "What happens when people disagree with you? What if you make a decision from the top and the masses below you say we don't believe in this?" And his response was, "People are going to do that anyway, and ultimately, the decision-making power, regardless of blogs or wikis or whatever, still rests within the infrastructure of the enterprise. No matter what tools you give your employees, you still have to give them a way to execute those decisions." In other words, the enterprise culture is what determines whether decisions are executed, not the technology.

Organizations that see a strategic value in being responsive to the concerns of their younger workers can use new technologies to provide open internal channels and an early-warning system for those at the top, as well as a means of feedback.

Developing Portable Skills   It is predicted that average Millennials will change careers ten times during their working lives. *Careers*, not jobs. The significance of this is not lost on the Millennials, who are focused on building a portfolio of skills that increase their value in the widest range of possible employment contexts. "They are very future oriented and are extremely eager to amass the cutting-edge skills they will need to increase their job market value," writes consultant Eric Chester.[47]

Millennials crave training, and they may need it in areas that earlier generations of workers did not. A 2006 report from a consortium of corporate leaders and industry organizations entitled "Are They Ready to Work?" discovered some alarming gaps in the basic preparedness of younger workers in the United States, even graduates of four-year colleges.[48] Public speaking, time management, and career planning are some of the skills in highest demand among younger workers,[49] in addition to remedial training in written communication and leadership, the most serious gaps identified by the consortium study.

Observers note that younger workers prefer to learn by doing, as opposed to traditional classroom-based training. This does not necessarily mean Web-based learning, which is actually less popular with workers in their twenties than among GenXers and younger Boomers, according to data published by the Center for Creative Leadership.[50] Millennial-age blogger Ryan Healy writes:

> At orientation, the first time my peers and I logged in to complete an e-learning course, we all looked at each other with puzzled faces. I thought, "Is this serious?" Others snickered throughout the whole assignment and most of us jumped through the course totally bored. *Without discussion or one-on-one teaching, e-learning is cheap, ineffective and gives the impression that a company does not care enough to invest time or money into training*—which in turn gives the impression that employees are unimportant.[51] [emphasis added]

When it comes to training Millennials, the what and the why are at least as important as the how. Organizations want and need to socialize younger workers into their particular culture and role-based practices, but evidence suggests that the information needs to be made specifically relevant to job performance, or Millennials (and GenXers) will tune it out. For example:

> "If you tell a person to stock a grocery shelf but to be cautious opening the boxes, he won't be," says Robert W. Wendover, director of The Center for Generational Studies, a research and training company in Aurora, Colo. "This person takes a box knife to open a case of Wheaties and slices across all the boxes. Then you have to discount that box. But, if you explain, 'In the grocery industry you only have a 1 percent profit margin, the box sells for $5, you're only making 5 cents, and by being forced to discount the box you have lost any profit that could have been made,' [this is how] you engage them. You need to teach them why they're doing what they're doing."[52]

Finally, recognize that *portable* skills are different from specialized skills. Millennials, for better or worse, often lack the patience to internalize information in depth and won't devote the time to master a skill that has a short shelf life, career-wise. They are quick to question the value of learning complex systems and practices that are likely to change rapidly or technology that displays obvious limitations.

Gaining Approval and Recognition Throughout the 1980s and 1990s, the American educational system sent messages of affirmation and validation to students, with the goal of building self-esteem through the celebration of each person's individual talents. At the same time, the economy sent another signal: be competitive or get out of the way. Millennials heard both signals loud and clear. They understand the necessity of contributing to a high standard and want to be acknowledged for their contribution. Many are also convinced that they have immediate value to add and are hungry for ways to make their voices heard, beyond the channels traditionally associated with entry-level roles.

"[Millennials] believe passionately that merit rather than length of service should drive promotion, progression and the acquisition of responsibility," writes Will Hutton in

Personnel Today. "They argue their Baby Boomer managers should acknowledge their demonstration of competence more fulsomely."[53]

Internal blogs and social networking sites can provide an informal, content-rich environment where employees can share knowledge in a public way, participate as equals in debates and dialogues, and create high-value personal connections within the organization.

Millennial Workstyle

The table below summarizes the implications of Millennial workstyles.

Millennial Workstyle	Culture Implication	Technology Implication
Connected	Greater emphasis on teamwork	Communication and collaboration systems, portals, workspaces, teamware, and tools
Multitasking	More dynamic, less structured environment	User environments that allow for shifting context
Visual and Interactive	Greater emphasis on visual communication rather than text-based content	Real-time visualization and modeling capabilities

Connected   Like Boomers, and unlike GenXers, Millennials often prefer working in teams, whether collocated or virtual. *Business Week* reports that "Even in school, solitary assignments have gradually given way to team projects. The result: a generation that feels most comfortable pursuing well-defined goals as part of a team."[54] This has obvious advantages in a large organization, and probably sounds especially appealing to Boomer managers who are weary of trying to mold prickly, team-averse GenXers into functioning business units. One by-product of this collaborative work ethic is that some Millennials are uncomfortable working alone or on self-directed assignments. They can also be averse to individual risk taking and fearful of personal accountability.

Organizations can support the upside of Millennial connectedness by furnishing the collaboration tools they are accustomed to using to build and sustain their networks. In addition to the real-time and mobile communication technologies discussed previously, this also includes team workspaces for document and project collaboration, cross-disciplinary communities as well as communities of practice, and expertise location systems to discover new people with whom to collaborate.

It can be expected that Millennials will have few, if any, cultural problems migrating personal documents and resources to shared repositories. They are generous with their information and connections, comfortable contributing knowledge in a variety of informal settings, and have fewer expectations of privacy in the connected workplace based on their experience on public networks and consumer sites. Organizations seeking to benefit from these values should find ways to reward and encourage open collaboration and be attentive to individual managers who model bad behavior by hoarding information.

Multitasking Distractions are the occupational hazard of the connected world. Older workers stress out, opt out, or burn out from information overload (a documented condition that has a cognitive impact twice as severe as smoking marijuana[55]). Younger people raised in an environment of perpetual stimulation have adapted by developing formidable multitasking skills that may even result in fundamental changes in the neural pathways of the brain.

According to the Pew Millennials study, 32 percent of IM users say they do other things on their computer, such as browsing the Web or playing games, *virtually every time* they are instant messaging, and another 29 percent are doing something else some of the time they are IM-ing.[56] It's not uncommon for young workers to be participating in several real-time interactions while performing routine business tasks, responding to e-mail, and listening to music on headphones. Managers (especially those with no day-to-day experience with Millennials at home) are likely to find such behavior disconcerting, if not disrespectful, at least until the young worker has proven that he or she is up to the job.

Futurist Douglas Rushkoff, writing in 1996, foresaw an upside to these unique attention-management capabilities:

> In the workspace of the future, a broader attention range and shorter absorption time will be valuable assets. The stockbroker with a broad attention range will be able to keep track of many markets at once as they flash by on his terminal. He will be able to talk on the phone to a client on one line, his boss on another, and an electronic chat on his computer screen, all simultaneously. His shortened attention span will keep him from getting too unconsciously engrossed in any one conversation or activity, and always ready for something new.[57]

Visual and Interactive Throughout the 1980s, 1990s, and 2000s, media imagery has become increasingly vivid and seductive. Computer animation in films is nearly indistinguishable from real-life photography. Each new advance in video gaming brings us closer to the experience of fully immersive virtual reality. Massively-multiplayer user domains (MUDs) online bring the complexities of human society into environments that exist entirely in the computer or network. Social-based avatar worlds like SecondLife take the experiential aspect to an entirely new level.

Not all Millennials are interested in these sorts of experiences; more than a few still lack access to the high-speed connections and high-performance platforms necessary to participate, although those barriers continue to drop lower almost daily. Still, immersive, visual, interactive media surrounds and permeates their lives, and offers a genuine, socially engaged alternative to reality that inner-directed escapes like drugs and spiritual mysticism cannot. The mere existence of this alternative changes expectations; to those who participate routinely in interactive games and simulated environments, it changes perceptions and rewires the machinery of consciousness in ways that educators and employers are only beginning to grasp. Marc Prensky writes:

> Digital Natives accustomed to the twitch-speed, multitasking, random-access, graphics-first, active, connected, fun, fantasy, quick-payoff world of their video games, MTV, and Internet are *bored* by most of today's education, well meaning as it may be. But worse, the many skills that new technologies *have* actually enhanced (e.g., parallel processing, graphics awareness, and random access)—which have profound implications for their learning—are almost totally ignored by educators.
>
> The cognitive differences of the Digital Natives *cry out* for new approaches to education with a better "fit." And, interestingly enough, it turns out that one of the few structures capable of meeting the Digital Natives' changing learning needs and requirements is the very video and computer games they so enjoy. This is why "Digital Game-Based Learning" is beginning to emerge and thrive.[58]

Some employers are recognizing the effectiveness of game-based learning for training and orientation. Nike, Ernst and Young, and Cisco Systems, among others, are experimenting with game-based training solutions that enrich traditional Web-based learning systems with richer interactivity, graphics, and video. "We thought about this audience for quite a while," said Michael Donahue, a program manager with Nike. "We knew the program had to be entertaining. A lot of these kids have grown up in the gaming era."[59]

WHY IT MATTERS: MANAGED
INNOVATION

The intimate relationship between Millennials and technology sets the stage for potential conflict within organizations that want to manage innovation in a more structured, disciplined way. Young workers are accustomed to open, informal communication, ad hoc collaboration, untethered mobility, vivid interactive applications, and immediate responsiveness. They have been using the technology that enables these things for their entire lives—as students, consumers, friends, and family members. The technology is effortless and nearly invisible to them, and it is fundamentally intertwined with their approach to problem solving, collaboration, and work.

When they come to work, many are disappointed to discover that their employers have no formal facilities or processes to enable the capabilities they rely on to be productive, or the flexibility they demand as a baseline requirement for job satisfaction. Because they don't necessarily view any particular job as an opportunity, much less a career, the technology shortcomings of a potential employer may weigh heavily as a factor in taking or keeping a job.

A 2006 survey of 250 Board-level executives of IT firms across the United Kingdom by the firm Unwired supports this conclusion. The report states that firms that fail to deploy the mobile technologies and flexible working practices desired by younger workers are in danger of failing to attract new talent. Young workers "now are so used to instant and informal communication that when they enter the workplace they will have very different expectations," said Richard Leyland, head of knowledge at Unwired. "They will expect access to technology to be mobile and available at any time," and see far less value in the traditional workplace, workday, or command-and-control hierarchy.

"When you talk to senior HR directors at blue-chip firms, their biggest challenge is how do they attract the bright 19-year-old who is going to graduate in four years with a good degree," said Leyland. "They know that if they don't get it right they will lose them to their rivals."

Unwired recommended that IT decision makers assess the effectiveness of their information management strategies with the workstyle priorities of Millennials in mind, arguing there needed to be a greater emphasis on retaining personal knowledge and sharing corporate information.

"People are going to move between different jobs more, so you need systems like corporate wikis that can capture employees' knowledge when they are with you," Leyland said. "You also need to realize that young people now live in a hyper-informal world and the culture of secrecy and tight information management evident at many firms needs to be relaxed." [60]

Unwired's approach represents one position: make the necessary changes and investments to accommodate younger workers, because you (and your competitors) need them more than they need you. There is another side to that argument, however. Many of these technologies are new and unproven in the enterprise, and businesses are not convinced of their value, assuming they even have the resources on hand to make the investments. Companies that do not have an early-adopter mindset may decide to wait for technology standards and implementation issues to sort themselves out, to avoid the risk of unforeseen costs or overinvesting in a dead-end strategy.

There's also a basic principle at stake for traditional organizations. The idea that the most junior workers in the organization would not only participate in, but actually influence and direct, important strategic decisions related to both business and technology is a radical inversion of the expectations that governed the 40-plus-year careers of many organizational leaders. The ability to set business priorities and practices is a management prerogative. Compliance is a condition of employment, not open to negotiation. Holding the line on these issues is seen as critical to maintaining discipline in the workplace.

Organizations can only succeed with this kind of strategy if they can get rank-and-file business users to buy in to the rationale behind the cautious approach to collaboration, transparency, and the supporting technology. That's because many of the most popular applications for instant messaging, social networking, blogging, file sharing, and distributed computing are widely and freely available on the Internet, where anyone can download and install them on their desktops or access hosted services from public Web sites. Organizations that do not have a formal infrastructure and policy around real-time communications may discover that employees (often, but not always, younger employees) have taken matters into their own hands by running Yahoo IM clients or hosting online meetings on public sites.

This is an extremely hazardous path to start down. From an IT perspective, consumer-grade Web 2.0 applications pose legitimate security, compliance, and governance objections, and when workers take it upon themselves to download these applications off the Web, install them on business computers, and use them in a business setting, they expose their employers to all manner of risks. Collaboration, multimedia, and data-sharing applications consume network resources and can hurt overall system performance. They add to IT support burdens and introduce unmanaged complexity and inconsistency into the information environment. Consumer-quality applications can put confidential data at risk through poor implementation of security features or through user behavior (e.g., sharing confidential or inappropriate content on informal systems) and put employers afoul of regulatory requirements for the control and retention of business information and communications. Some applications downloaded off public networks contain malware that directly threatens enterprise security. In addition, some IT professionals are convinced that many of these applications serve either a very limited business purpose or none at all, and generally hurt employee productivity rather than enhance it.

A 2006 report from the American Management Association and the ePolicy Institute contained some sobering data about the scope of the problem. According to the survey of 416 companies representing a cross-section of sizes and industries:

- While 35 percent of employees use IM at work, only 31 percent of organizations have an IM policy in place, and only 13 percent retain IM business records.

- While 50 percent of workplace users report downloading free IM tools from the Internet, 26 percent of employers have no awareness of the use of IM in their organization.

- Significant numbers of employees report using IM for jokes (26 percent), gossip, rumors, and disparaging remarks (24 percent); confidential company, employee, and client information (12 percent); and sexual, romantic, and pornographic chat (10 percent).

- About 8 percent of organizations operate business blogs; 9 percent have policy governing the operation of personal blogs on company time; 7 percent have policy governing employees' business blog use and content; 7 percent have rules governing the content employees may post on their personal home-based blogs; 5 percent have anti-blog policies banning blog use on company time; and 3 percent have blog record retention policies in place.

- One-quarter (26 percent) of employers have terminated employees for e-mail misuse; 2 percent have dismissed workers for inappropriate IM chat; and nearly 2 percent have fired workers for offensive blog content—including posts on employees' personal home-based blogs.[61]

In a 2006 survey reported by Sophos, a network security firm, 86.4 percent of IT administrators expressed the desire to block unauthorized IM applications in their enterprises, with comparable numbers also opposed to Voice over IP (VoIP), peer-to-peer file sharing, distributed computing applications, and games (over 90 percent opposed). Between 60 and 79 percent of respondents said that blocking such applications was "essential."[62]

This is a fight management can win in the short term. Organizations can and do set limits on permissible practices and sternly discipline or dismiss employees who violate company policies. IT can lock down the information work environment by preventing the installation or use of unauthorized applications, blocking inbound or outbound network access to unapproved sites, and monitoring employee communications down to the keystroke. Management can hold the line on investments in unproven Web 2.0 technologies and stick to vertically oriented portals and specialized applications rather than broad-based enterprise collaboration tools and less formal types of applications that users prefer.

Organizations should understand that, in a multigenerational workforce aspiring to attract, retain, and motivate wired Millennial employees, these are not simply IT policies, but also human resource policies. They send a clear message about the way the organization values the workstyle, priorities, and potential contributions of younger workers. As the skills shortage deepens over the next 10 to 15 years, organizations will need to take a more holistic view of their IT policies in the context of the overall need for skilled, productive, but demanding Millennials in the workforce.

Can Millennials live without IM, blogs, and social networks at work? Of course. Will they still work for employers who don't equip them with the latest and greatest stuff to allow them to achieve the work/life integration they say they want? Some will, at least until they pay off their student loans and credit card debt, or get a better offer. However, in a competitive global environment, it's not about the minimum you can get away with; it's about the maximum you can achieve. Young workers empowered with collaborative technology can be enormous creators of value, as can workers of any age. Young workers motivated by a workplace that respects their autonomy and supports their life and work priorities will be an asset to their employers for years to come. Young workers will support management decisions and respect boundaries if organizations take the time to explain the context and the rationale.

OUTLOOK

Embracing the workstyle of Millennials does not mean wholesale compromise of good management principles or haphazard adoption of potentially risky IT solutions, but it does mean starting a broader dialogue about business and IT issues. Chapter 8, Listening to the Future, explores how one company sought out the views of Millennials to gain strategic insights into the future of the workforce.

ENDNOTES

1. Howe, Neil, and William Strauss. *Millennials Rising: The Next Great Generation*. New York: Vintage, 2000.
2. Yglesias, Matthew. Matthew Yglesias Blog. The Atlantic.com, 2007. http://matthewyglesias.theatlantic.com; and Klein, Ezra. Tomorrow's Media Conspiracy Today Blog, 2007. http://ezraklein.typepad.com, respectively.
3. According to the U.S. Census Bureau.

4. Rattner, Lizzy. "The New Victorians." *The New York Observer*, July 15, 2007.

5. "How Young People Lead Their Lives: A Portrait of Generation Next." Pew Center for People and The Press, January 9, 2007. Andrew Kohut, Director. Note that this study polled those ages 18 to 25 (b. 1981–1989).

6. Bryson, Lew. "Deadly Serious." Lew Bryson's Buzz Blog, The Buzz: A Beerfly's View, April 2007. http://lewbryson.com/buzz0407.htm

7. Howe, Neill, and William Strauss. "Will the Real Generation Y Please Stand Up?" *The Los Angeles Times*, March 2, 2007. http://www.latimes.com/news/opinion/la-oe-howe2mar02,0,4956647.story?coll=la-opinion-rightrail

8. "The Movement Toward Community Colleges." Online Newshour Report, June 19, 2006. www.pbs.org/newshour/generation-next/demographic/college_06-19.html

9. Ernst and Young, Canada. "Sixty-five Per Cent of College Students Think They Will Become Millionaires." 2001. Press Information Worldwide. March 14, 2005. www.pressi.com/us/release/35870.html

10. Quoted in Jayson, S. "Generation Y Makes a Mark, and its imprint is entrepreneurship." *USA Today*, December 8, 2006.

11. *Ibid*.

12. Trunk, Penelope. "How to Reach the New American Dream." Brazen Careerist Blog, posted June 26, 2006. http://blog.penelopetrunk.com/2006/06/26/how-to-reach-the-new-american-dream/

13. "The 11th Biannual Youth Survey on Politics and Public Service by Harvard University's Institute of Politics," November 1, 2006. www.iop.harvard.edu/pdfs/survey/fall_2006_execsumm.pdf

14. Pallavi, Gogoi. "Welcome to the Generation Y Workplace." *Business Week*, May 4, 2005. www.businessweek.com/bwdaily/dnflash/may2005/nf2005054_4640_db_083.htm

15. Martin, Carolyn, and Bruce Tulgan. *Managing Generation Y: Global Citizens Born in the Late Seventies and Early Eighties*. Amherst: HRD Press, 2001.

16. "Twenty Five Years of the IBM PC." BBC News, August 11, 2006. http://news.bbc.co.uk/2/hi/technology/4780963.stm

17. Ennefils, Diane. "Number of Personal Computers in the US." Edited by Glenn Elert, *The Physics Factbook*™, 2004. http://hypertextbook.com/facts/2004/DianeEnnefils.shtml

18. Pew Center for People and the Press, January 9, 2007.

19. Junco, Reynol, and Jeanna Mastrodicasa. *Connecting to the net. Generation*. NASPA, 2007, p. 65–82.

20. Windam, Carrie. "Father Google and Mother IM: Confessions of a Net Gen Learner." *EDUCAUSE Review*, 40.5, 2005, p. 42–59.

21. Prensky, Marc. "Digital Natives, Digital Immigrants." From *On the Horizon*. Lincoln: NCB University Press, Vol. 9, No. 5, October 2001.

22. Pew Center for People and the Press, January 9, 2007.

23. *Ibid.*

24. Jayson, Sharon. "The Millennials Come of Age." *USA Today*, June 29, 2006.

25. Trunk, Penelope. "Moving Back Home with Your Parents Is a Good Career Move." Brazen Careerist Blog, posted May 15, 2005. http://blog.penelopetrunk.com/2005/05/15/moving-back-home-with-your-parents-is-a-good-career-move/

26. Dychtwald, Ken et al. *Workforce Crisis*. Boston: HBS Press, 2006, p. 104.

27. Hira, Nadira. "Attracting the Twentysomething Worker." *Fortune*, May 28, 2007. http://money.cnn.com/magazines/fortune/fortune_archive/2007/05/28/100033934/index.htm

28. Quoted in Jayson, S. "Generation Y Makes a Mark, and its Imprint is Entrepreneurship." *USA Today*, December 8, 2006.

29. Reported in *New Scientist*, April 7, 2007.

30. Lenhard, Amanda et al. *Teens and Technology: Youth Are Leading the Transition to a Fully Wired and Mobile Nation*. Pew Internet and American Life Project, July 2005.

31. "Teens and Media: A Full-time Job." CNET, December 7, 2006. www.news.com/2100-1041_3-6141920.html

32. *Managing Generation Y: Global Citizens Born in the Late Seventies and Early Eighties*, p. 22.

33. Pew Center for People and the Press, January 9, 2007.

34. Meeham, Emily. "New Grads Quickly Grow Impatient for Promotions." *Wall Street Journal*, June 22, 2007.

35. Trunk, Penelope. "New Financial Data Highlights Generational Rifts." Brazen Careerist Blog, posted May 29, 2007. http://knowledge.emory.edu/article.cfm?articleid=950

36. "Generation Next Changes the Face of the Workplace." Online Newshour Report, December 14, 2006. www.pbs.org/newshour/bb/business/july-dec06/geny_12-14.html

37. Tyler, Katherine. "The Tethered Generation." *HR Magazine*, May 2007. www.shrm.org/hrmagazine/articles/0507/0507cover.asp

38. Hershatter, Andrea, and Molly Epstein. Reported in "Is Your Firm Ready for the Millennials?" 2006. http://knowledge.emory.edu/article.cfm?articleid=950

39. *Op Cit.* Hira.

40. Op Cit. Ernst and Young Canada, p. 4.

41. "Work-life Integration = New Hotness." Millennials at Work Blog, May 5, 2007.[41]http://millennialsatwork.wordpress.com/2007/05/05/work-life-integration-new-hotness/

42. *2006 Cone Millennial Cause Study.* Cone, Inc. with AMP Insights, October, 2006.

43. *Op Cit.* Tyler.

44. Havenstein, Heather. "Facebook Users Resisting Wal-Mart's Latest Web 2.0 Endeavor." *Computerworld*, August 27, 2007. www.computerworld.com/action/article.do?command=viewArticleBasic&articleId=9032718&intsrc=news_ts_head

45. Stiglitz, Joseph. *Making Globalization Work.* New York: W.W. Norton & Company, 2007, p. 199.

46. The phone interview between the author and Oliver Young took place on July 9, 2007.

47. Chester, Eric. Employing Generation Why? Understanding, Managing and Motivating Your New Workforce. Lakewood: Tucker House Books, 2002.

48. "Are They Really Ready to Work? Employers' Perspectives on the Basic Knowledge and Applied Skills of New Entrants to the 21st Century U.S. Workforce." The Conference Board, Inc., The Partnership for 21st Century Skills, Corporate Choices for Working Families, and The Society for Human Resource Management, 2006.

49. Deal, *Retiring the Generation Gap*, p. 184.

50. *Ibid.*

51. Healy, Ryan. "Throw away e-learning." Employee Evolution Blog, May, 15, 2007. http://www.employeeevolution.com/archives/2007/05/15/throw-away-e-learning/

52. *Op. Cit.* Tyler.

53. Hutton, Will. "Wear Kid Gloves When Tackling Generation Y." *Personnel Today*, 2003, p. 17.

54. "The Best Places to Launch a Career." *Business Week*, September 18, 2006. www.businessweek.com/print/magazine/content/06_38/b4001601.htm?chan=gl

55. As reported in *The New Scientist*, issue 2497, April 30, 2005. www.newscientist.com/channel/being-human/mg18624973.400.

56. Shiu, Eulynn, and Amanda Lenhart. "How Americans Use Instant Messaging." Pew Internet and American Life Project, September 1, 2004. www.pewinternet.org/PPF/r/133/report_display.asp

57. Rushkoff, Douglas. *Playing the Future: What We Can Learn from Digital Kids.* New York: Riverhead Books, 1996, p. 51.

58. Prensky, Marc. "Listening to the Natives (Digital Immigrants, Digital Natives Part 2)." From *On the Horizon*, Lincoln: NCB University Press, Vol. 9, No. 6, December 2001.)

59. Rose, Barbara. "Generation Y Plays Games on the Job." *The Seattle Times*, May 20, 2007. http://seattletimes.nwsource.com/html/businesstechnology/2003714122_geny20.html

60. Murray, James. "IT Chiefs Must Prepare for Informal 'Generation Y.'" *IT Week*, January 16, 2007. www.itweek.co.uk/itweek/news/2172595/chiefs-prepare-informal

61. 2006 Workplace E-Mail, Instant Messaging & Blog Survey, cosponsored by American Management Association (www.amanet.org) and The ePolicy Institute (www.epolicyinstitute.com). www.indystar.com/assets/pdf/BG76179610.PDF

62. *Instant Messaging, VoIP, P2P, and Games in the Workplace: How to Take Back Control.* Sophos, Inc. 2007.

～6～

Generation X-ecutive: Leadership from the Outside In

For the past 25 years, as organizations have adopted increasingly sophisticated connected information work technologies in the workplace, senior leaders have mostly been drawn from the ranks of those who came of age before the dawn of the PC revolution. Today, the first generation that saw computers before they graduated from high school is poised to join the ranks of executive management in increasing numbers. These are the 51 million members of Generation X, now moving into their thirties and forties, starting families, and looking to stamp their imprint on society and the economy as mature adults. In their younger days, GenXers gained a reputation for independence and skepticism. Many pursued careers as free agents and entrepreneurs—either out of choice or because traditional career paths were not open to them. Now, with waves of retirements opening up leadership opportunities, seasoned GenXers provide organizations with a strong combination of pragmatic problem-solving ability and deep understanding of technology that can bridge the gap between aging Boomers and rising Millennials.

As in the case of older workers, the midcareer bracket actually straddles two generations with different values and approaches to practically everything except technology. Late-wave Boomers, born 1955 to 1962, are in many cases already established in leadership roles as they arrive at their career peaks. During the PC revolution and the build-out that followed, these younger Boomers were the visionaries and evangelists of new technology, leading companies that saw their missions in terms of big ideas: social transformation, personal empowerment, global interconnectedness. As workers and consumers, late-wave Boomers learned to use computers and devices as adults, mastering successive waves of new capabilities and new complexities and combining those skills with the Boomer work ethic and high level of organizational commitment, in contrast to the detached reluctance of many GenXers.

The combination of Boomer vision at the top, GenXer pragmatism in executive and middle management, and Millennial can-do spirit in the ranks of up-and-coming workers makes for a very positive alignment of generational strengths and organizational roles, provided that the generations can harmonize their workstyles around a common approach to technology and the practices that support its use in the workplace. Midcareer workers—both Boomers and GenXers—are the operational front lines for the implementation of key technology decisions, and the leaders or leaders-in-waiting who have to manage the multi-generational workforce of the next 20 years. To fulfill that role, they need to look beyond their own experience as the creators, masters, and target consumers of new technology and recognize how invisible biases in technology and the policies surrounding its use can create points of friction between generations.

LATE-WAVE BOOMERS

Younger Boomers (b. 1955–1962), sometimes referred to as "Generation Jones,"[1] share many of the values and assumptions of their elders but came of age under somewhat different historical circumstances. Too young to participate in the Civil Rights marches of the early 60s, experience the Summer of Love or Woodstock firsthand, or to be subject to the draft, young American Boomers reached their late teens in a period of cultural exhaustion and drift. They were still products of the postwar consumer culture, still optimistic and full of high ideals, but they arrived at the big party just as it was heading into its weird late-night mode. If the early Boom was typified by JFK's Camelot, the Beatles, and Lenny Bruce, the late Boom was Watergate, Led Zeppelin, and Saturday Night Live. The unfortunate 1961–1964 (late Boom–GenX cusp) cohort also represented the nadir of American postwar academic achievement and the highest incidence of measurable social pathologies (violent crime, substance abuse, teen pregnancy, premature death) throughout the first quarter of their life cycle.[2]

The great cultural touchstone of the early Boom was the assassination of President Kennedy. For slightly younger late Boomers, it was the *Apollo* moon landing in the summer of 1969—an exciting triumph of human ingenuity and technology. As the second wave of the Boom came of age in the 1970s and found that their older brothers and sisters had already exhausted the most obvious possibilities of social and political change, a select few took inspiration from the achievements of Veteran and Silent NASA engineers and sought to realize their transformative vision through technology. On college campuses throughout the mid-70s, Boomer idealism combined with the increasing capabilities and falling costs of semiconductors, the development of more powerful computer programming languages, and the nascent network of academic mainframes that later evolved into the Internet. The result was a culture of *hackers*— young computer scientists who sought to make the towering number-crunching machines of the early information age into something less forbidding, more fun, and scaled to the needs of people, not just organizations.[3]

The whole idea of a "personal computer" was nearly unintelligible to the Veteran-generation managers running corporate IT departments and university computer labs. It was like saying you wanted a "personal ocean liner" or a "personal power plant." Even if such a thing were technically and economically feasible, what possible purpose could it serve? It took the imagination of young Boomers like Steve Wozniak (b. 1950), Steve Jobs (b. 1955), Steve Case (b. 1958), Paul Allen (b. 1953), and Bill Gates (b. 1955)[4] to see the potential of the computer as a tool for personal empowerment rather than a piece of industrial equipment, and to relentlessly pursue their vision until it was both a practical reality and a viable business.

Young Boomers who weren't leading the PC revolution were among the fast-followers. Although most were not trained technologists or engineers and did not see computers in the course of their education, they were new to the workforce in the early 1980s when the first IBM PCs were coming into use. They were also at low rungs of the organizational ladder, in roles where they were more likely to appreciate the convenience of a word processor or spreadsheet program, because they could not rely on a secretary to type up their memos or a staff of accountants to recalculate numerical forecasts. Workers without technical backgrounds were nevertheless motivated to learn and master the often-difficult first-generation interfaces, because the payoff was the power and autonomy that came from having control over information.

This early experience of empowerment made an impression on late Boomers (and some first-wave Boomers who understood the dynamics of the situation) and cemented their roles as the innovators, early adopters, and evangelists of technology in the workplace and the wider world. Even as they head into their fifties, late Boomers maintain their enthusiasm for the transformative effects of information access, and have consolidated their power after two or more decades in positions of leadership across the IT profession and the technology industry.

GENERATION X

Generation X is the common designation for the cohort between the Boomers and Millennials, taken from the popular 1991 novel of that name by Douglas Coupland.[5] Strauss and Howe called them the 13th Generation (because of their luckless historical timing and the fact that they were, by their reckoning, the 13th generation born in America).[6] Experts place the first birth year of Generation X as early as 1960 and as late as 1965. For the purposes of this book, I chose 1963, the year that birthrates in the United States—already in decline since the late 1950s—took a nosedive, owing at least in part to the introduction of the birth control pill. GenX birth years extend to 1980; 1981 is the consensus date for the first birth year of Millennials. That puts the number of GenXers in the U.S. population at around 51 million, compared to 78 million Boomers and 80 million Millennials.

GenXers are more ethnically diverse than previous generations (though not as diverse as Millennials): in the United States, 37 percent are nonwhite, compared to 27 percent of Boomers and 20 percent of Silents.[7] Many had mothers who worked outside the home. The share of women participating in the labor force who had children under the age of six jumped from 18.6 percent in 1960 to 59.9 percent in 1992.[8] During most of the 1970s and 1980s, family size in America declined from 3.3 children during the Baby Boom to 1.9 children during the birth years of Generation X (since risen to around 2.08 during the Millennial era). Approximately 40 percent of their parents divorced.

GenXers were children at a time when Boomers were pushing cultural limits as teenagers and young adults, and when many social, economic, and political trends in the United States were heading in a downward direction. A number of dire predictions hovered over them in childhood, from the exhaustion of natural resources and the perils of overpopulation, to the pronouncement that they would be the first generation in history to have lower economic prospects than their parents (a prediction that is coming true in the case of GenX men, according to a 2006 study).[9]

The personal computer arrived just as the oldest GenX-ers were entering their adolescence in the late 1970s. Unlike most other things in the culture during those years, computers worked according to comprehensible rules and were getting demonstrably better all the time. The new PCs were immediate and interactive—different from the teletype and timeshare systems in common business use at the time. Popular, affordable models such as the Apple II and the Radio Shack TRS-80 ran word processors, spreadsheets, games, and other software, but their main appeal was that they could be programmed to do computations, graphics functions, and even music using accessible languages like Basic, Pascal, and LOGO.

Curious GenXer teens pushed the limits of early PCs, often motivated by the desire to get their more limited desktop computers to emulate the vividness of popular arcade video games, which were a step ahead in graphics and processing power. Some users became adept at security protocols by hacking the copy protection schemes used to prevent unauthorized duplication of commercial games and software, or learned networking skills by setting up bulletin-board systems to chat, gossip, and share software.

These sorts of activities pushed the computer proficiency of teens far beyond the level of their teachers and parents. When the first computer-savvy GenXers appeared in the workforce as entry-level employees and interns in the mid-1980s, employers took note of their skills and comfort with office PCs, which often sat idle and ignored, or were used as dumb terminals connected to mainframes. Not only did GenXers bring a higher level of basic competence with computers as a result of school classes, but they also had a deeper understanding of how the computer was supposed to work, which made it easier for them to learn and customize new software and discover new applications for computer technology that older IT planners hadn't considered.

The initial impact of GenX in the workplace was blunted by turbulent conditions in the 1980s, a decade that saw recessions, a stock market crash, the last terrifying moments of the Cold War, economic upheaval, political realignments, and the outbreak of the AIDS epidemic. The first GenXers to emerge from four-year colleges in the mid- to late-80s graduated into a recessed economy and had difficulties finding work in their fields that Boomers only a few years older did not.

These historical and cultural circumstances helped form the hard-edged and independent generational character of the GenXers. From birth, society's message to them was "you're on your own." They spent most of their early years looking up at a growing heap of social, political, environmental, and economic problems that glib Boomers appeared more interested in arguing about (and making worse) than actually solving. GenXers grew impatient with the fatuous spirituality and utopianism of their Boomer teachers and cultural figures, and with the modest, nonconfrontational style of their Silent generation parents. As they entered their adolescence and young adulthood, their rebellion took the form of rejecting both idealism and compromise, instead looking to create their own subculture communities that reflected their authentic experience, as opposed to Boomer commercial culture, which seemed increasingly detached from reality. Technology, as it turned out, was a large part of those subcultures. Rap music featured computerized beats and cutting-edge digital production; do-it-yourself (DIY) media like 'zines and public-access TV capitalized on new low-cost digital desktop publishing and video production technology; rave culture was fueled by electronic music and psychedelic computer graphics, and was celebrated in early-90s technophile artifacts such as *Mondo 2000* magazine.

By the early 1990s, technology proficiency was a core component of the distinctive GenX identity and became part of the cultural discourse. Douglas Rushkoff was only one of several GenX authors who propounded a unified-field theory of an aesthetic, spiritual, political, and organizational paradigm shift based on the transformative effects of computer networks and GenXers' unique relationship to them.[10] Just as the main body of GenX was entering the workforce in the 1990s, economic and political conditions in the world began to change for the better, partly because of the transformative impact of new information and communication technology. The U.S. economy improved under a new administration, not only bouncing back from the depths of recession, but also racing forward with the creation of new jobs, new business, and entire new industries. The maturation of low-cost computer technology set the stage for one of the most entrepreneurial periods in recent economic history, and many of the GenXers who couldn't find the first rung on the corporate ladder just a few years earlier decided to strike out on their own.

Throughout the anything-goes 1990s, young GenXers were risk takers and adventurers. In business, they were the dotcom entrepreneurs like Amazon's Jeff Bezos (b. 1964) and eBay's Pierre Omidar (b. 1967), and software mavericks like Netscape developer Marc Andreesen (b. 1971) and Linux creator Linus Torvalds (b. 1969). In the wider culture of the 1990s, they were superstars of individual achievement like cyclist Lance Armstrong (b. 1971) and skateboarder Tony Hawk (b. 1968), and creators of accusatory and self-referential art and music like the late Nirvana frontman Kurt Cobain (1967–1994), rap musician turned comedy actor Ice

Cube (b. 1969), actress/activist Janeane Garofalo (b. 1964), or graphic novelist Chris Ware (b. 1967). GenXers were the bike messengers and perma-temps, the post-feminist, late-marrying free agents, and the skeptical, hard-to-reach consumers. Companies wondered how to market to them[11]; employers resorted to all manner of novelties to attract, retain, and motivate them.

Then the curtain came down. By 2001, the dotcom economy had crashed, along with the freewheeling GenX workplace of foosball games, Aeron chairs, and laptop docks for nomadic employees (at least temporarily). The events of 9/11 led to a more polarized and security-conscious cultural environment, far less permissive of individual expression and risk taking. A triumphalist Boomer ideologue administration took charge in Washington, and their top prewar priority was to distribute the budget surplus in the form of tax cuts, rather than hold it in trust to alleviate the looming entitlement crisis whose brunt, many GenXers knew, would likely fall on them. GenXers who joined the armed forces in the 1990s and early 2000s as a way to gain job skills and life purpose have had to put their careers and family lives indefinitely on hold as they fight the wars that arose from the American response to the terrorist attacks.

Although the cultural spotlight moved on (perhaps to the GenXers relief) to the more camera-friendly Millennials, the GenXers, of course, didn't go away. Now in their thirties and early forties, they are starting families, taking on mortgages, participating in community and political activities—some of them are even writing books. They are moving inexorably into the prime of their working lives and beginning to look for ways to do the work that will define their careers and establish themselves as firmly in the economy as their opulent Silent parents and extravagant Boomer elders.

GenX IN THE WORKFORCE

The generational personality of GenXers has made them problematic employees from the perspective of older managers. They are largely unmotivated by team purpose like the Veterans (and now, the Millennials), by technocratic dedication like the Silents, or by lofty ideals and work-for-work's-sake like the Boomers. They resist sentimental attachment to their work and put their own interests first, because they expect that organizations will eventually betray and abandon them, as they did to their parents during waves of downsizing since the 1970s.

Entrepreneurial and Independent: Recruitment and retention of GenXers has been difficult, although for most organizations it will seem like merely a dress rehearsal for the impending issues surrounding Millennials. Relatively large numbers of GenXers prefer self-employment or entrepreneurship and have made it work as a career choice at a far earlier stage of life than other recent generations. In a 1995 survey, Babson College Professor Paul Reynolds found that "10% of Americans between the ages of 25–34 are actively involved in creating a start-up company, a rate about three times as high as any other age group.... It should help dispel once and for all the myth that today's youth are motivationally challenged."[12]

That entrepreneurial trend has accelerated as GenXers have gained experience and relationships in the workforce. According to a 2004 survey of more than 1,000 GenXers by American Demographics:

> Gen X respondents classified themselves as Self-employed Professionals 25 percent more frequently than did their older counterparts in the survey, and 10 percent of Gen X respondents said their title was Owner-Partner. Rather than swearing fealty to a large corporation, 38 percent of Gen X respondents said they worked for privately held companies or for a private individual,

while only 18 percent said they were employed by a publicly held company.[13]

Resourcefulness is the byword of the entrepreneur, and it is a value cherished by GenXers, whether they are self-employed or part of larger organizations. GenXers are drawn to solutions—including technology—that give them high leverage to make the most of their limited time and energy. If a portable phone is good, a phone that is also a PDA, a music player, an Internet browser, and a global positioning device is even better. GenXers don't prefer complexity per se, but many are willing to take the time to learn a more complex piece of software if it gives them greater ability to control their work environment, manage more stuff with less effort, or dispense with a low-value task so they can do something more interesting.

Work/Life Balance: GenXers have always prioritized personal time over work and are continuing to do so as they transition into family life and parenthood. As of 2004, GenXers were raising more than half of all children under 18 in the United States, some 40 million kids.[14] While the concepts of the "latchkey kid" and "quality time" typified the approach of Boomer and Silent parents to raising young GenXers in the 70s, grown-up GenXers who are determined to give their children a different type of family experience have popularized the concepts of "stay-at-home dad" and "flextime." More GenX dads are leaving work to raise kids, working from home, or cutting back long hours than previous generations. Although GenX women are more college-educated than any previous generation, more GenX moms have opted to stay home or work part time, reversing trends among Boomer women.[15]

Nearly all workers express a desire for more balance between work and life, but this issue is near and dear to the hearts of GenXers because of their life stage and their generational outlook. GenXers are avid fans of telework technologies, both because they reduce the time they are required to spend in the arbitrary confines of the workplace and because they give people more control over how they divide their time between work and life activities. As GenXers ascend into management ranks, telework solutions must be more than a thin tether of voice/e-mail connectivity to the office. They must provide richer access to more workplace resources: secure virtual private network (VPN) access to enterprise data systems and shared workspaces; rich, real-time communication channels for face-to-face interactions and virtual meetings; the ability to replicate the workplace desktop anywhere, without too much overhead of synchronization; remote management of IT resources, and so on.

The societal benefits of telecommuting, which include potential reductions in traffic, fuel consumption, auto emissions, and time lost in transit, are compelling. Home- or remote-based work provides access to the workforce to people with limited mobility and increases the lifestyle choices available to individuals and families who potentially no longer need to choose between proximity to the workplace and convenient schools, affordable housing, open space, cultural infrastructure, or other social amenities they deem important.

All of the pieces to the telework puzzle are finally in place, except one: management buy-in. While acceptance of telework has been steadily on the rise, significant numbers of managers admit they find the presenteeism mindset hard to break. According to a 2007 British study,[16] managers trust remote workers to be productive when they are out of sight, but still have greater regard for those who show up and visibly put in long hours at the office. In addition, 44 percent of the managers polled said they were unprepared for the supervision of remote teams, and only one-quarter had received any training on how to manage such a team.[17] This attitude isn't restricted to management, either. A 2005 survey by IBM's Institute for Business Value and the Economist Business Intelligence Unit found that nearly 40 percent of European workers felt that their colleagues working from home were slacking off, whereas more than 60 percent of home-based workers felt they were doing more and being appreciated less.[18]

The relationship between showing up and working hard is sheer common sense to Boomer managers, whose entire work experiences have been defined primarily by attendance, face-to-face interaction, and workplace culture. They can intellectually recognize the potential (and actual) value of telework, but the emotional connection and trust form more slowly. Workers recognize this issue, and even those who might benefit immensely from the convenience of working from home may be reluctant to fully embrace the opportunities.

From a generational perspective, telework is at odds with the defining characteristics of the Boomer workstyle—the importance of personal contact, group politicking, the need to make a conspicuous display of hard work and commitment, and the need to manage teams and colleagues through direct supervision—although it emphatically supports the stated priorities and workstyles of younger workers. Even Boomers who desperately want to enjoy the greater flexibility and reduced costs of working remotely may feel conflicted about the consequences that not showing up might have on their perceived value and commitment. And they wouldn't be wrong: a 2007 study by Los Angeles–based recruitment firm Korn/Ferry International found that 61 percent of executives (in all probability, mostly Boomers) believe telecommuters have lower chances of career advancement than colleagues who work in the office—yet nearly half of the 1,320 executives polled also said they would consider a job that involved regular telecommuting.[19]

As the values of GenX gain currency in the executive corridor, it is very likely that organizational cultures will become more accommodating of telework models, even at the expense of the benefits of collocation. Several GenX small business owners I spoke to for this book expressed an enthusiastic preference for remote work as a defining aspect of their workplace culture, as well as an important aspect of their personal workstyles as the parents of young children. Frequently, the technology to support people working from home is among the first investments they make. They manage to performance, not attendance, and hire workers who are comfortable and productive with that model.

Working Smarter and Harder: One reason that work/life balance is such an issue for GenXers is that they are working longer, harder, and for less. Early in their careers, GenXers got a reputation as slackers for their lack of commitment to the Boomer work ethic and their reluctance to internalize the values of their employers. As they enter midcareer, GenXers are now among the hardest-working cohorts in the workplace, especially those in management. Only 26 percent of managers reported working less than 40 hours per week in 2007, with 65 percent averaging 41 to 60 hours, and 9 percent putting in more than 61 hours, according to a report by Randstaat Work Solutions. Of employees polled in the study, 24 percent say they put in six or more hours per week without pay.[20]

The relationship between time and productivity is crucial to GenXers, who understand that economic results are tied to outputs, but who nevertheless remain interested in spending as little time as possible on activities they do not consider central to their life priorities or values. GenXers prefer to work toward defined objectives and resent management that prioritizes time-consuming process over results. "Freedom-loving Xers resent the corporate compulsion to have meetings about meetings," write Lancaster and Stillman in *When Generations Collide*. "They hate to be micromanaged, and struggle to understand why it's so important for someone to see them if they are getting the work done satisfactorily."[21]

Many of these traits are also what make GenXers singularly productive and valuable as individual contributors and entrepreneurs. In a competitive environment that prizes efficiency, GenXers have become masters at finding shortcuts that save time and effort. Penelope Trunk, columnist and author of *Brazen Careerist*, writes on her blog: "Our dreams are tied to time.... And topics like productivity are favorites among hipsters who know that 'getting things done' (GTD in blog-speak) is the key to having a fulfilling life. And believe me, GTD doesn't take money, it takes massive respect for one's time."[22]

As such, GenXers tend to be attracted to the labor-saving benefits of technology and annoyed by features that disrespect one's time by demanding too much unnecessary interaction in the name of user-friendliness. To a GenXer, it's worth the time to create a macro or script to automate a common task, even if that requires expert-level knowledge of the software. RSS feeds and podcasts are attractive, because they reduce the need to surf out to Web sites and instead just serve the information up automatically. This desire to solve a problem once and then not have to think about it again—born out of a generational obsession with efficiency and practicality—tends to put GenXer managers at odds with Boomers, who revel in the gritty details of personal interaction, and with Millennials' insatiable curiosity to understand the strategic importance of every management tactic and task.

MIDCAREER WORKERS: TECHNOLOGY CREATED IN THEIR IMAGE

The centrality of computer technology to work represents a rare meeting of the minds between idealistic younger Boomers eager to accomplish big transformative projects and pragmatic GenXers eager to squeeze out pointless inefficiencies so they can get back to their real lives outside of work. Both generations grew up with computer technology, although GenXers encountered it in their childhood and early teens, while Late Boomers first saw it as young professionals in the mid-80s.

Late Boomers and GenXers tend to have the fewest issues with technology because the technology was, by and large, created by them,[23] for them. As IT professionals and power users in business settings, they have adapted computers, software, and networks to their workstyles and priorities. As consumers in the desirable 25 to 55 demographic, they have driven the market for particular combinations of design and capabilities in high-tech gadgets and software, most of which find their way into business settings sooner or later. Their tastes and values—influenced in many ways by generational factors—are encoded into the DNA of the information environment at a level so deep that they can seem invisible, but in fact, they may constitute one of the most significant factors in the technology age gap. Consider these examples:

- *Productivity software* is packed with features and menus to give users the widest range of capabilities and the greatest number of options to personalize their work experience. Though most users rarely venture beyond the most basic level of features, the design principle of "more is better" fits both the Boomer conception of value and the GenX imperative to prepare for any contingency. Users who have learned the conventions of the interface from earlier versions of the products know how and where to find the features they need and how to customize the applications to fit their workstyle. In fact, many vendors assume the practices are so widespread that they do not bother shipping printed documentation with their products.

- *Mobile devices* keep getting smaller and have metastasized from basic telephones into multifunction devices and veritable portable computers for resourceful GenXers and gadget-happy Boomers. They look like the communicators and tricorders popularized on *Star Trek*, a favorite of Boomers and GenXers alike. The menu structure of phones is intuitive to people with experience using desktop computers. The small buttons and tiny displays pose fewer inconveniences for users whose eyesight and manual dexterity are not yet diminished by age.

- *Instant Messaging* and text messages sent from mobile devices are full of abbreviations designed to spare the sender the inconvenience of typing out additional characters on an awkward keyboard. This has created a kind of texting jargon that is famously impenetrable to most adults, and evolves so quickly that it's amazing even teenagers can keep up with it. IM and texting are also aggressively abrupt and informal, as e-mail can be—technologies used and created by Boomers and GenXers with no use for empty pleasantries or the formalities cherished by pre-Boomers.

- *Blogs and wikis* create an environment where unofficial and uncredentialed contributors stand at eye level with traditionally authoritative sources of knowledge. This is perfectly natural to GenXers, who believe that performance and competence should be the sole criteria for authority, and who are tired of looking up at entrenched Boomer elites who, in their view, owe their positions to politicking and ideological affiliation.

- *Work/life balance* in its current conception supports Boomer always-on workaholism and GenX cravings for flexible scheduling. It is, however, essentially a one-way flow of work into life. Organizations remain skeptical, if not hostile, to Millennial conceptions of

work/life integration that involve bringing life interests and relationships into the workplace, especially if
it comes in by way of insecure and hard-to-manage
technologies like social networking, podcasting, and
blogging.

In each of these cases, it is possible to imagine the frustration of tech-forward Boomers and GenXers if the biases
were reversed: if the only mobile phones available were
enormous to accommodate big screens and buttons, or if
the standard version of office software were only available
with limited functionality so people would not be anxious
about having to learn so much new material. Instead, the
aesthetics of small, complicated devices and the willingness
to trade simplicity for functionality fit the generational priorities of young Boomers and GenXers to a tee.

It may seem unfair to lay the quirks and shortcomings
of modern technology at the feet of an entire generation
(or generation-and-a-half), when those directly responsible
were a relative handful of technology professionals in the
employ of a small number of high-tech companies. However, there is an important lesson applicable to broader issues of leadership in the experience of young Boomers and
GenXers in the software design and engineering profes-
sions.

Interface design guru Alan Cooper convincingly (and
hilariously) argues in his 1999 book *The Inmates Are Running
the Asylum*[24] that software developers are a breed apart from
ordinary people, with a far greater willingness to tolerate
complexity and frustration in exchange for knowledge and
control. This is reinforced by the conditions under which
programmers do their jobs:

> Programmers have a strong sense of insularity and what it im-
> plies. Nobody can have significant control over what a pro-
> grammer does inside his own program. Programmers know
> that the quality of their code is largely a matter of their own

conscientiousness. The boss can demand quality, but the boss isn't going to invest more time to decipher the programmer's code than it took to originally write it. Programmers know this, and they know that their personal decisions and actions have more leverage on the final product and the user's satisfaction than any other consideration. . . . When marketers, managers, or designers give advice to them, programmers regard the advice with a healthy dose of skepticism.[25]

What's striking is how the values and culture that Cooper ascribes to programmers—independence, obsession with efficiency as a way to save personal time and effort, low priority on interpersonal communication skills, focus on outcomes rather than process (such as meetings or showing up on a regular schedule), seeing risk in a positive light, desire to dominate through competence—sound like the thumbnail descriptions of Generation X tossed out by management analysts:

Xers will sidestep rules and procedures that slow them down as they push for results. They're willing to take risks and innovate —even when it drives their older bosses crazy.
    —Martin and Tulgan, *Managing the Generation Mix*[26]

They show up late, leave early, and appear to be "slackers" because they are keeping their eye on what they think is the ball—getting the work done.
    —Zemke, Raines, and Filipczak, *Generations at Work*[27]

For Boomers, face time is a strategic tool, but Xers see it as a waste of time, or, put more frankly, an attempt to kiss up to the boss for no reason.
    —Lancaster and Stillman, *When Generations Collide*[28]

Assuming that these generalizations are broad-based and not drawn exclusively from the ranks of GenXers in the high-tech industry or in IT roles, it seems that many GenXers in the working world have internalized the transactional values and habits of engineers and applied them to other aspects of their personal and business lives. Obviously, most GenXers outside the engineering profession don't have the rigorous training and precise habits of mind typical of professional technologists. Many GenXers, however, share a belief that their generational experience growing up independent during a troubled socioeconomic era in American history gives them a privileged perspective (even expertise) on the realities of life that pampered Boomers and Millennials lack. They look down on Boomers who rally to high-minded motivational slogans and see employment as an expression of their inner values rather than a simple economic transaction, and are befuddled by the Millennials' enthusiastic embrace of teamwork and commercial culture. Like engineers, they prefer to keep their approach to issues rooted in reality—even unpleasant reality—because in the end, only the cold facts determine outcomes.

WHY IT MATTERS: BECOMING LEADERS

The quantitative, transactional mindset of engineers is well-matched to the realities of a results-driven, bottom-line world, as members of GenX doubtless learned while observing the meteoric rise of software businesses and the bright career prospects of software developers during the 1980s and 90s. Engineers espouse an extreme form of unsentimental rationality well-suited to a global free market that picks winners and losers on the sole basis of performance. Such a worldview is also a convenient, effective antidote to Boomer idealism, which many GenXers find pompous and self-deceptive.

The downside is that the cult of competence prevalent in the engineering culture demands a lot from end users—and this is equally true of the stereotypical GenXer worldview. When the designers of products (or the managers of business processes) personally value self-reliance, process efficiency, abrupt communication, and transactional relationships, they tend to impute those values to everyone else and criticize those who fall short. The products and processes they design are rich in features that reward the deep knowledge and expertise of power users, but are short on user-friendly flourishes that engineers consider wasteful. This bias runs deep in the high-tech industry, where unsophisticated users, rather than antisocial designers, are often seen as the problem. Typically, a software company or device maker will spend millions in product support to assist confused customers rather than invest in a simpler, more usable design in the first place. Organizations run according to these sorts of principles will likewise spend considerable time, money, and effort to engineer business processes, and then invest again in getting processes to run as intended, because their designers did not pay sufficient attention to intangible people-centric issues.

This goes right to the issue of leadership. Boomers recognize the value of consensus, discussion, and human values in business, even if they tend to overdo it in the eyes of some older and younger workers. GenXers have characteristically demonstrated impatience with social niceties and prefer the most brutally simple path from point A to point B. Unlike Boomers, they see work primarily as transactional—a means to achieving other life priorities, rather than a priority unto itself. According to the values and experience of GenXers, the convenience and freedom afforded by technology innovations are high; the frustrations of adapting to new products and processes are relatively low, since they have been doing it from an early age anyway; and the sacrifices of intangibles like face time and culture are meaningless, since those values were largely superfluous to their view of work in the first place.

As executives, GenXers will be empowered to make those kinds of decisions on behalf of their entire organization rather than just themselves. And, like engineers, they may be tempted to assume that their values are shared by those at the other end of the process. Manifestly, they are not. Pretending otherwise, no matter how compelling the logic might seem, is a recipe for exacerbating rather than ameliorating workplace tensions that can reduce productivity.

For their own reasons, neither Boomers nor GenXers are well-equipped to see the forest for the trees. Boomers, even the younger ones, are accustomed to redefining society according to their norms and values. They've been doing it since birth. The process is invisible and natural to them. GenXers, having survived on their wits and seen their skepticism validated by events and the failures of Boomer ideology, tend to equate their personal values and coping strategy with realism and practicality, which renders alternative views less realistic and practical by implication. Late Boomers and GenXers in management positions may be prone to dismissing the very notion of generational bias in technology in the same way that engineers minimize design flaws in their products by claiming user error.

OUTLOOK

As organizational leaders, Boomers and GenXers can galvanize the intergenerational workforce into an unprecedented engine of productivity, innovation, and responsive service. Their personal facility and familiarity with technology can be a huge asset. They just need to be cautious about projecting their own values and priorities into the workplace through their technology choices and strategy, without first taking the time to bridge the digital age gap through practices, dialogue, and cultural adaptation that accounts for diversity across all of the generations at work.

ENDNOTES

1. A term coined by author Jonathan Pontell.

2. Strauss and Howe, *Generations*, p. 52.

3. For an excellent history of this era, see Levy, Steven. *Hackers: Heroes of the Computer Revolution*. New York: Dell Publishing, 1984. This theme was later picked up in Markoff, John. *What the Doormouse Said: How the Sixties Counterculture Shaped the Personal Computer Industry*. New York: Penguin Books, 2005.

4. Founders of Apple, AOL, and Microsoft, respectively.

5. Coupland, Douglas. *Generation X: Tales of an Accelerated Culture*. Coupland did not coin the term—it was the name of a 70s-era punk rock band fronted by Billy Idol.

6. Howe, Neil, and William Strauss. *13th Gen: Abort, Retry, Ignore, Fail?* New York: Vintage, 1993.

7. U.S. Census Bureau, Census 2000.

8. Statistical Abstract of the U.S. Department of Commerce, 1993, pp. 152–155.

9. Sawhill, Isabel, and John Morton. "Economic Mobility: Is the American Dream Alive and Well?" The Pew Charitable Trusts Economic Mobility Project, 2006. www.economicmobility.org/assets/pdfs/EMP%20American%20Dream%20Report.pdf

10. Rushkoff, Douglas. *Playing the Future: What We Can Learn from Digital Kids*. New York: Riverhead Books, 1996.

11. For an amusing account of Boomer ad execs trying to pin down GenX as a target market, see Wice, Nathaniel, "Generalization X," in Rushkoff, Douglas, *The GenX Reader*. New York: Ballantine Books, 1994.

12. *U.S. News and World Report*, September 23, 1996.

13. Reynolds, Christopher. "Generation X: The Unbeholden." *American Demographics*, May 1, 2004. http://findarticles.com/p/articles/mi_m4021/is_4_26/ai_n6052824

14. DeMarco, Laura. "Gen X Turns Out Some Grade A Parents." *The Oregonian*, September 12, 2004.

15. *Ibid*.

16. "Tomorrow's Leaders: Managing Teams Remotely." City & Guilds and the Institute of Leadership & Management (ILM) in conjunction with Peter Thomson, Future Work Forum, Henley Management Centre, July 2007. www.cityandguilds.com/documents/Tomorrows_Leaders_Report_Kim.pdf

17. Paton, Nic. "Managers Still Suspicious of Home Working." *Management-Issues*, July 30, 2007. www.management-issues.com/2007/7/30/research/managers-still-suspicious-of-home-working.asp

18. Reported in Amble, Brian. "Remote Workers Suffer from 'Trust Gap.'" *Management-Issues*, May 13, 2005. http://www.management-issues.com/2006/8/24/research/remote-workers-suffer-from-a-trust-gap.asp

19. Reported in Perelman, Deborah. "Execs: Telecommuting Holds Back Careers." *eWeek*, January 18, 2007. http://www.eweek.com/article2/0,1895,2085460,00.asp

20. "The World of Work 2007." Randstat USA/Harris Interactive, 2007.

21. Lancaster and Stillman, *When Generations Collide*, p. 114.

22. Trunk, Penelope. "How to Reach the New American Dream." Brazen Careerist Blog, posted June 26, 2006. http://blog.penelopetrunk.com/2006/06/26/how-to-reach-the-new-american-dream/

23. Between 1989 and 1999, the computer and data processing industry was the nation's second fastest growing, as it added more than 1 million jobs over the period, an increase of 149 percent. Most were filled by GenXers or younger Boomers.

24. Cooper, Alan. *The Inmates Are Running the Asylum: Why High Tech Products Drive Us Crazy and How to Restore the Sanity.* Indianapolis: SAMS/Macmillan, 1999.

25. *Ibid,* p. 118.

26. Martin, Carolyn, and Bruce Tulgan. *Managing the Generation Mix.* New Haven: Rainmaker Thinking, 2006, p. 43

27. Zemke, Raines, and Filipczak, *Generations at Work*, p. 100.

28. Lancaster and Stillman, *When Generations Collide*, p. 114.

~7~

Reintegrating Older Workers into the Connected Information Workplace

Chapter 4 discussed some of the barriers facing older workers attempting to rejoin the workforce without the high level of technology skills, comfort, and intuitive familiarity necessary to fully participate in the connected information workplace. The question for these workers is not whether they can or cannot learn the basics; obviously, they must do so in order to be viable candidates for any information-work position. But the kind of training and acculturation they receive can help determine whether they view their information tools as a necessary evil or as a powerful way to refresh their careers and project their experience into a valuable new context for their employers.

This is an issue primarily affecting a certain category of older workers: those transitioning from careers, economic or educational backgrounds, or lifestyles that did not expose them to mainstream information work applications or practices, and who find themselves on the outside looking in at the whole culture of technology. It may also include older adults who were able to keep up to a certain point, but then gave up in frustration as their work became more dependent on complicated technology and less about the job they thought of as their career. Although this group comprises millions of people in the United States alone and many more around the world, this class of workers can be easy to ignore for those already inside the high-tech bubble, especially younger decision makers who are comfortable with, and largely responsible for, the rapid pace of change. After all, a tech-savvy manager might ask, "What can these people possibly contribute if they don't even know how to use the Internet?"

Lots, as it turns out. In a competitive market for skills and talent, they represent a new source of value that organizations can turn to for expertise, a familiar work ethic, and a mature perspective, especially as skills grow scarce and expensive. Industries run according to more traditional models, such as shipping and logistics, agriculture, and energy are increasingly relying on older workers because of difficulties attracting Millennials to "old economy" jobs or developing new leadership from within. Industry groups including the Society for Human Resource Management, and advocates for older workers such as the American Association for Retired People (AARP), already provide a vast number of resources to support workforce development, retraining, and placement of older workers, and are tireless advocates of the benefits of employing veteran workers in important roles. Still, in the end, it is up to the people themselves to adapt to the tools and culture of the connected workplace. If they can be motivated to succeed and surmount the generational barriers to participation, the benefits to themselves and their employers are clear.

In this chapter, we will meet some of these people firsthand and explore the successful methods that one organization has developed to smoothly integrate them into today's connected information workplace.

THE DIGITAL AGE GAP

The digital divide isn't news. It's been around for at least 20 years, though it has usually been expressed in economic, rather than demographic, terms. The difference today is that workers don't just need fundamental competence in software anymore. The increasing sophistication and connectivity of the information workplace means that people need to internalize a whole set of values and practices associated with the application of technology to work. If you grew up around computers, use the Internet every day, and embrace the underlying benefits of flexibility, decentralization, transparency, immediacy, and informality that come with the daily barrage of communication and information, then adapting to the dynamics of the connected workplace is an easy step. For some deeply wired Millennials and GenXers, the high-tech workplace is even a step backward from their normal lifestyle.

But for people who grew up in the predigital world and have not evolved with the technology in the workplace for the past 20 years, connecting to the new world of work is a much bigger leap. Organizations that want to use the considerable talents of these people need to find ways to help them bridge the gap. What they find, however, is that standard training and orientation programs are often not effective. They convey information, but not in ways that are useful or relevant to older adults, and they ignore the cultural issues rooted in generational values and workstyles that pose the real barriers to full participation.

The culture of technology conspires to make outsiders feel stupid and incompetent, almost by design. The language we use to talk about computers and technology is lush with jargon and acronyms. Devices and software are filled with hidden features, accessible only if the user has some prior understanding of the way the product is supposed to work. Commonplace consumer products come with hefty user manuals; software applications these days rarely do. Part of the marketing of new technology depends on the supplier making the customer feel that older products and older skills are useless and out of date and will put the owner at a competitive disadvantage unless they are upgraded. It is easy to see how organizations could come to apply that attitude toward the people who use the technology as well as the technology itself.

In fact, it is possible that the people who are annoyed and intimidated by complex technology are the ones understanding the problem correctly. The things that can go wrong with technology are numerous and increasingly obscure. It can be difficult for a nonexpert to determine whether a problem is something easily recovered from or potentially fatal. The complexity of systems creates a Catch-22 for people who are stuck, as it can be difficult to even describe the problem accurately. The experience of interacting with a help desk can be confusing, time-consuming, unpleasant, and ultimately *un*helpful.

These problems plague technology users of all ages. GenXers and Millennials, who have experienced the growing pains of various high-tech devices and software firsthand, recognize glitches when they see them and often take a skeptical view toward the claims of vendors. They are comfortable with their skills, and when technology goes awry, they assign the blame to incompetent developers, lousy product design, and flawed business models—which are, indeed, often the culprits. Those without knowledge or confidence, however, blame themselves for being too stupid to figure out a gadget that is, after all, not really for or about them anyway. If forced into contact with difficult technology in the workplace, those with low comfort levels will look for ways to avoid using intimidating systems or participating beyond the bare minimum in knowledge-sharing activities. And, as discussed in Chapter 4, it can be uncomfortable for older workers to seek help from younger colleagues or subordinates because of issues related to control, authority, and social dynamics.

Even people with great determination to master technology to improve their employment opportunities have trouble penetrating this thicket of difficulties, especially when the technologies at issue represent a culturally unfamiliar approach to things like collaboration or content development. Training programs meant to convey information can actually compound the problem by reinforcing the perception of complexity or making the students feel self-conscious about their lack of prior knowledge. If these issues correlate to age and differences in generational learning styles and are not accounted for in the way the class is set up, training meant to narrow the digital age gap can end up reinforcing stereotypes, discouraging older workers, and making it more difficult to manage a multi-generational workforce.

SERVING THE TECHNOLOGY NEEDS OF OLDER ADULTS

Older Adults Technology Services (OATS)[1] is a New York–based nonprofit with several years of practical experience overcoming exactly these challenges. Founded in 2003 by activist, educator, and entrepreneur Thomas Kamber, Ph.D., OATS defines as its mission to engage, train, and support older adults in using technology to improve their lives, and increase their civic and social engagement. It builds on the efforts of similar organizations around the country, and on the momentum for senior empowerment in workforce development championed by advocacy groups like the AARP. Since its inception, OATS has graduated several thousand older adults age 50 and up from three levels of

10-week technology training programs that it offers, and has run workshops and one-day seminars for thousands more.

Kamber is passionate about his organization's mission to reach out to the broad community of older adults in New York City, from all ethnic, educational, and economic backgrounds. While he acknowledges that older seniors and those from lower-income communities tend to have the greatest demand for technology services, he notes that many well-educated, experienced workers in their fifties and sixties also lack fundamental computer skills and have not been well-served by training programs in their workplace or community that are geared to younger, more technoliterate generations.

OATS runs classes at community centers, retirement communities, and various spaces in New York City that provide computer and network facilities. The curriculum currently includes three tracks: basic computer skills, workforce development (office applications), and advanced Internet (search, blogs, wikis, basic HTML), and there is some discussion of adding a fourth track to cover graphics, photography, music, and multimedia. The classes comprise no more than 15 participants and run 75 minutes twice per week over 10 weeks. OATS instructors are chosen for their classroom skills and personal approach rather than their technical knowledge. They receive special training and orientation, and are often assisted by community youth volunteers (ages 13 to 20), who receive school credit as part of the OATS intergenerational program.

Workforce development training for older adults is a major component of the OATS program. According to Kamber, close to half the people who come to OATS and ask for computer classes are thinking about working, are currently working, or would like to be more engaged in their communities and feel that technology is the key to that.

"We had a woman come in last year who was working in a professional office as a realtor and was finding herself slipping farther behind the other realtors because she couldn't use the technology," says Kamber. "She was so upset and even embarrassed about this that she called me and said 'I'd rather you not let the real estate agency know or call my agency and talk to me about the class because I don't want them to know that I'm having so many problems with the computer, but I really would like to improve my skills.' She came to us because it was having a very direct effect on her. She was losing money because of it. We get a lot of older adults like that—people coming from jobs where they only had to know a little bit of technology to do their job and then start finding that their offices were becoming more technology-heavy and they just got pushed out. They would have stayed working longer and felt like they could contribute more if they were able to adapt to the computer changes."

Renée Martinez is an instructor and project manager for OATS. "What we found was we had a lot of retired people who wanted to get back into the workforce," she says. "They wanted to have Microsoft Word experience or Microsoft Excel classes. And when they went to the library and took a one-day Microsoft Word class, it was too advanced. There wasn't a specific curriculum designed for them. And so we developed this class. Most of the students that I have in the class are retired city workers, people who drove a bus for 30 years, or they worked in a bank—not really around technology—and then they retired and realized they're living a lot longer. They retire at 60 or 65. They have another 20 years of just sitting around. And some of the other students that I have in there, it's about 50 percent of retirees and then probably 30 percent of people who are still in the workforce who don't want to get pushed out, or they sit down in front of a computer and they are asking their younger peers, 'How do I do this? How do I forward

this e-mail? How do I make this column bigger in Excel?'
So they find themselves relying completely on the younger
staff in order to do their work."

LEARNING STYLE OF OLDER ADULTS

"Older adults do learn a little bit differently about technology," says Kamber. "They bring different strengths and
weaknesses to the process. That categorically seems to be
the case across all of the older people that we're working
with." One core principle of OATS is that technology training for older adults will be more successful if it plays to their
strengths and squarely addresses the weaknesses unique to
members of the predigital generations.

Immediately upon establishing OATS, Kamber and his
staff undertook a research study to identify the specific factors that lead to the success or failure of technology training
programs for older adults. One thing they found is that older
workers and retirees were primarily enrolling in continuing
education programs or signing up for classes at community
colleges, and were not satisfied with the quality of instruction. "They were having a hard time learning at these local
sites principally because they were moving too quickly. The
courses went very fast, especially with the preliminary material."

He surveyed the work of other organizations across
the country, conducted extensive discussions with seniors
and educators, and looked critically at the different ways
that older people sought out technology information. The
OATS team identified gaps in existing programs and set
out to develop an educational approach that incorporated
design principles specific to the learning styles of older
adults.

Kamber believes that much of what they've learned
is transferable to corporate and government organizations

and small businesses, in addition to other nonprofit and community groups. "One of the things that we've learned is that this work that we're doing is something that requires a high degree of professionalization," says Kamber. "Other organizations have tried for years to teach computer classes to seniors using volunteer workers, volunteer labor, low-wage occasional folks who come in as consultants, and are getting paid to just teach the computer classes and they're using the *Computers for Dummies* book or something like that. And it's treated almost like 'Oh, we'll just do a little program on that, and it will be something good for the seniors.' That is patronizing and, in fact, it doesn't engage people and the materials aren't appropriate for them, the trainers don't have the skills, they're not recruited for the kinds of capabilities that we look for, and ultimately that's left a lot more frustrated people out there feeling like, 'Oh, you can't teach seniors.'"

Kamber says that OATS has learned that if you create a system that is designed for older adults and respects them, they will learn and make remarkable progress. He says the OATS approach combines a defined learning and education methodology, practice, feedback, evaluation, recruitment, and management, provides people with high-quality materials in comfortable training environments, and treats this as a professional challenge on a par with any other kind of training or workforce development initiative.

FIRST STEPS

Over three years, OATS has extended and developed the curriculum, incorporating changes to the software and technology and integrating lessons learned from classroom experience. Despite the constant refinements, OATS sticks to a few key principles that have contributed to their success:

- Don't neglect the basics
- Use content relevant to older adults
- Attend to ergonomic and economic realities
- Go slow, go deep
- Support linear learning with documentation
- Reduce the frustration threshold

Don't Neglect the Basics: A major objection many older people have with traditional technology training programs is that classes they took often began by assuming a certain level of skill and familiarity with basic computer functions such as the mouse and keyboard. OATS trainers point out that a lot of older people, especially men, never learned to type or had to do much typing in their jobs, so the keyboard is not their friend. They also point out that the mouse can be difficult to learn at first if people are not used to the idea of interactivity. "It's not a natural connection for some people to assume that moving a mouse on a table or desk makes something happen on the screen," observes Kamber. When instructors fail to recognize the challenges that some older people might have learning a new motor skill involving hand-eye coordination, they make older students feel slow and inadequate for having difficulties with a critical function that their instructors consider too elementary to even discuss.

Dee Derr-Daugherty, program director for OATS, has designed technology training curricula for youth, midcareer workers, and seniors. "When we develop the curriculum for older adults, we break it down to the very basics and go step by step," Derr-Daugherty says. "For instance, we teach people how to use the mouse. It sounds easy for someone who is used to it, but you have to teach them how to move it, how to click, double-click, what the different cursors look like and what they mean." Derr-Daugherty emphasizes that it requires a lot of patience and a lot of repetition.

However, once users are comfortable, it is much easier to move on to more advanced material because students are not distracted by feeling self-conscious about their difficulty doing something that they know other people consider extremely basic.

"Older adults understand information architecture, they understand the Internet and the complicated material," says Renée Martinez. "The trouble is the input device. I think a lot of people don't expect that, and so it's not part of their training approach."

Older adults with more computer experience than the average OATS student may not have the same specific problems with the mouse or input device, but the principle remains the same. Whatever the subject matter, start at the beginning: don't assume a great depth of prior technology knowledge (even among educated people or experienced workers), and don't move on until the students have mastered the fundamental techniques.

Use Content Relevant to Older Adults: Kamber says that computer training programs geared to younger people miss the mark with older adults for several reasons. "Some of the content is completely inappropriate for older people," says Kamber, noting that many classes use examples drawn from popular culture or sites of interest to youth and teens, which turns off older adults and reinforces the idea that the technology is not designed for them.

OATS seeks out content and exercises of immediate interest and relevance to their users. "When we do Internet research, we do medical research, travel research, and things like that as a basis and then we cover what they're interested in," says Derr-Daugherty. Tasks center on things like résumé preparation, using the Web to look for jobs, social and professional networking, and using multimedia tools to find music and video geared to the tastes of older adults.

Attend to Ergonomic and Economic Realities: OATS found that the physical environment of the computerized office can pose barriers to entry for older people. Even the ergonomics of the community computer labs they began using were designed for younger people's bodies and younger people's threshold of comfort. OATS learned to address that issue early on, in a way that acknowledged the challenges faced by people as they age without making them feel self-conscious or singling them out. The classes also accommodate older adults with physical limitations. "A lot of people don't like to admit that their eyesight isn't what it used to be or they have trouble sitting for long periods," says Derr-Daugherty. "We spend the first few moments of the class acknowledging those differences. We recognize that people aren't going to learn as well if they can't see the board or can't read the text on their monitor."

Economics are also a concern. In the course of the preliminary research, OATS discovered that many training programs start from the presumption that students would have access to high-end computers and high-speed Internet connections at home to practice lessons learned in the class. "Many older people are very budget-conscious," says Kamber. "They are skeptical of investing in expensive equipment or paying for DSL service until they know they can use it and get value out of it." OATS has therefore designed the curriculum to be self-contained within the classroom and computer lab and has looked to remove economic biases and excessive technology requirements.

Go Slow, Go Deep: OATS found that instructional programs for older adults are successful when they play to a unique cognitive strength of older adults: the ability to process and retain volumes of technical data when it is presented slowly, clearly, and in sequence. "Older adults bring to the table a lifelong amount of experience and knowledge that they've accumulated about topics, especially technical topics," says Kamber. "When you interact with them, they often want to go quite deeply into the information."

This finding is backed by recent studies, including a survey of air traffic controllers, which found that older people retain technical information better than younger people, despite being somewhat less agile in dealing with material presented in rapid-fire succession. The studies also found that older workers have strategies for managing that information that are actually more effective than the strategies that younger people employed. [2]

The key to enabling long-term retention is to start slow and reinforce constantly. "At the beginning of each class, I spend at least five minutes reviewing concepts," says Martinez. "It's extremely important to have patience, especially in the early going." OATS has found that while older students may have difficulty getting a concept the first time or even the fifth time, when they get it, it has taken root at a very deep level.

Support Linear Learning with Documentation: While younger people learn technology by hands-on experimentation and trial and error, Kamber and his team find that older learners prefer information in step-by-step instructions and value written documentation.

"Older people don't learn the way the Web is designed," says Martinez. "The Web is designed so you can get to places through 100 different ways; it's nonlinear. But older adults learn in a very linear fashion. They grew up where you do step one, step two, step three, step four, end result. And so a lot of them, they'll look at their neighbor's screen and say, 'How come his screen doesn't look like mine?' They're looking at the same information, but it may look a little bit differently because of the way their browser is set up or their screen resolution. It's confusing because they are used to thinking that there is a right and wrong way to do everything. So a lot of the things that we teach, we have to somehow come up with a way to break it down one, two, three, four. Sending an attachment—this is how many steps it takes to send an attachment. Things like that need to be linear for them to understand, at least until they are used to the way the systems work."

"People joke about this," says Kamber, "but when you give a group of 65-year-olds a document about the computer, you will find a lot of them really poring over that and reading it very carefully and absorbing the information and really banking that information."

OATS provides detailed workbooks and documentation that covers all material from each lesson in step-by-step form. Explains Kamber, "We find that with older students, you can present them with a long piece of text that a 25-year-old or 40-year-old would find just too impenetrable or daunting. And a 60-year-old will sit down and read it happily and absorb and retain that information. So as we teach the classes, I'm finding that we can go a lot deeper in some of the topics that we teach. And we're finding that people really engage us that way. There's just a longer attention span."

Reduce the Frustration Threshold: Kamber uses the term "frustration threshold" to describe the negative reaction he has observed of many older adults toward technology they see as unduly complex and overbuilt for its intended function. "When an older person starts working with a phone, computer, or digital device and they don't succeed quickly in learning how to use it, they run into a stumbling block or something doesn't turn out the way they expected it to, they become frustrated very quickly compared to a younger person," he says. Whereas a 15-year-old will keep playing with it until they have made some progress, older users are quicker to blame themselves for breaking the device or failing to understand some simple function. They get frustrated and give up, usually with a bad feeling about the experience and technology in general.

The low frustration threshold, combined with negative messages about technology in the media around such issues as identity theft, viruses, and malware, make it very stressful for people with limited familiarity and understanding of technology in the first place. Rather than deal with the stress, they simply opt out. The frustration threshold is a significant barrier as technology increases in complexity and number of features.

OATS deals with the frustration threshold problem by setting expectations realistically in advance. "Computers do break," says Kamber. "There is such a thing as the 'blue screen of death.' Programs sometimes lock up and you need to restart the computer—not every five minutes, but once in a while. So giving older users a realistic sense of what to expect, what to look for, and how often things break is part of the solution."

The second part of the approach is to give older users a buddy to help them get comfortable with the technology. OATS training sessions feature a lot of hands-on experimentation, but at the outset, it is supervised closely by the instructor or a young volunteer. When students encounter a problem, the instructor provides immediate context about whether it is serious or just a quirk of the system, and provides simple, nonjudgmental assistance on how to recover. "We've created an active community of people face to face in a room with each other, learning the technology together. The anxiety level that people feel is reduced," says Kamber. "It is not the kind of thing where you can give somebody a CD-ROM and say 'plug this into your machine and follow the instructions, then call me when you're finished.' That works great with younger people who feel comfortable or actually prefer learning on their own, but it's absolutely the wrong approach with older adults."

MOVING BEYOND THE BASICS

Training inexperienced people in the basics of computer operation is a necessary precondition to integrating (or reintegrating) them into the information workforce, but the real success of the OATS program is the way it provides people who did not grow up with digital technology, and who often feel disconnected and intimidated by the culture of technology, with the confidence and orientation to become active participants in extremely advanced knowledge environments.

Cheryl Mahnis, 57, works in merchandising for a major New York department store. Prior to that, she was a freelance editor for educational publishers, and earned a master's degree from San Francisco State University. Though she had limited experience with specialized retail systems at work, she had no knowledge of basic PC technology, office applications, or the Internet. "I knew nothing about computers and it was hard to learn from people who were very experienced," she explains. "I realized that this is the way of the world and you feel very left out if you can't participate."

Looking for a change at work, Mahnis signed up for the OATS basic class, then followed with the workforce development program, and enrolled in the advanced Internet skills class in the summer of 2007. "Before I came here, I barely knew how to turn a computer on," she says. "It's expanded my whole world." Mahnis attributes her success to the patience of the instructor and the way that the program made her and her classmates feel comfortable at each step of the way, despite their initial lack of even rudimentary knowledge. Whereas in the past, she would have been reluctant to try to learn applications on her own or participate in training with more tech-savvy younger people, she now feels she could hold her own. "I would definitely feel comfortable," she says. "Prior to that, I would never even have considered it."

Once she realized that the doors to the digital world were open to her, Mahnis sought out ways to contribute her insights. As part of the OATS advanced Internet class, she is using a Web-based content development tool to build an online employment resource for older adults, hosted on the OATS Senior Planet Web site. "I'm working on providing information on job opportunities for retirees who might want to go back to work full time, or part time, people who might be interested in changing careers," she explains while demonstrating the use of the Wiki-based application she is using to create the listings. "I've been exploring Web sites that are available, then putting the links on the site with a brief description."

Thai Jason, 62, is enrolled in the workforce development class. She recently retired after 27 years of running a firm that produces musical jingles for advertising, and currently works part-time for ReServe, an agency that places qualified seniors with nonprofit organizations. Though she worked at a high level in a technology-intensive workplace and industry, she personally never acquired mainstream information work skills. "You know, I had a computer on my desk," she explains. "I think it's a classic example among a certain kind of person. I had young people all around me who grew up with computers, they were really good and two things happened. Number one was, you know, I'd write a letter or something and say to my assistant, 'make this look good,' and she would take it away and bring it back and it was gorgeous and I signed it. The second thing is that when I actually wanted to learn something, it felt like nobody had the patience. Everything was running fast. People said, 'I'll just do it for you.'"

After several failed attempts to get training and tutoring, Jason discovered OATS. Not only did she find the pace of the class and the patience of the trainers more to her liking, she also found it easier to learn in an environment with other older adults. Once she found her footing, she made rapid progress. "I go back to the office and I'm actually using the stuff I learn in the class immediately," she says. "And I'm getting kudos for it from my young fellow workers."

Perhaps the biggest breakthrough is that Jason now feels free to learn on her own, using the same explore-and-discover techniques that younger people use to teach themselves advanced features of the software. "I think a lot of people who didn't grow up with the computer have this fear, which is that 'Oh, my God, I'm going to lose it!' You know, it's all going to go away, and I'll break it, it will be my fault, and if it disappears from the screen it's gone forever. You know, those are classic fears, and I think that we've been shown techniques so that we can get it back, and that you haven't lost it. So because I know that now, I have been exploring some of the buttons and bells and whistles that I didn't know before what they were."

BRINGING SKILLS AND EXPERIENCE TO THE CONNECTED WORKPLACE

The reason that some older workers still lack proficiency with computers and productivity software is that they have spent the majority of their careers in roles that have not seen much, if any, exposure to digital technology. They might be coming out of occupations that require expert skills and advanced education, such as teaching or nursing, or from operational roles in manufacturing, transportation, construction, agriculture, mining, and so on, where it is entirely possible to retire from a 30-year career at age 50 and still have many potentially productive years ahead.

What these types of workers lack in established information work skills, they make up for with firsthand, front-line experience, and maturity, in addition to the work ethic and commitment typical of the Boomer generation. While an inexperienced employee may be able to find information to apply to a business problem somewhere in a database or network, the veteran may have a more reliable solution at hand based on a richer understanding of the situation. As competition heats up for younger workers with ready-made information skills, organizations may find that a comparatively small investment in training older, nontraditional information workers with the necessary skills is money well spent for several reasons.

Vivian Notturno, 56, drove a school bus for 23 years and did routine office administration tasks in an environment that did not use computers. "I got to a point after 22 years of driving the bus where it was doing some damage to my back," she says. "Sometimes you have a feeling that if you're 56, you know, you're not going to be employable, or it's too late, you might as well just stay at the job you're at. And it really has an effect on you, being an older person. Once I got past that and I realized that middle age now is 65, and, you know, I am marketable, I am very bright, and I am willing to take risks."

She recognized that she needed computer skills to widen her options, but was discouraged by her prior experiences with training programs. "My experience, when someone tried to teach me the computer, is that they would be doing everything. And that would frustrate me because they would be doing it so fast and I just would feel very overwhelmed and very confused, and it would just validate the fact that I just can't do this. OATS was not like that. OATS would take time and they just let us do it over and over and over until we got it. And when we did get it, you could just see us light up and be so excited about being able to do these simple things that other people just took for granted, like, 'Oh, you should know this.' And it changed my life. It really did. It gave me self-esteem; it made me feel really good about myself. It made me feel good about my peers that I was in the class with and it really made me see how important it is for older people to get this opportunity."

Notturno says she soon got her résumé in order and began networking. Before long, she landed a job as benefits coordinator for First Transit, a transportation company affiliated with the Metropolitan Transit Association (MTA) in New York, working at the command center. "The reason why First Transit was interested in me is because I had 22 years background in transportation," she says. "I worked my way up from the bottom, so I had a lot of experience in transportation and personnel. The piece that was missing was the computers."

Her employer was willing to train her to use the specialized forms and templates necessary to her role as benefits administrator. This went quickly and easily because Notturno had gained both competence and confidence as a result of her prior experience with OATS. She says she has no hesitation participating in more advanced training at work or figuring out how to use unfamiliar applications by applying her existing skills. She works closely with coworkers and has no problems asking for help or, increasingly, furnishing computer advice to her colleagues.

BECOMING COMFORTABLE IN THE DIGITAL CULTURE

Many older people don't live in a world where their peers talk about technology issues or exchange information about new high-tech products and services. They are not a primary market for technology vendors; advertising campaigns are not created around their tastes and values; and marketing does not appear frequently in media that they regularly consume. As a result, they have far less exposure to the ambient stream of background data that informs the views of younger people about technology, and fewer clues to help separate good questions from ones that would reveal their lack of knowledge and sophistication. This runs counter to both their experience and their expectation that age should give them *more* insight and wisdom rather than less, as it does on most other life issues.

For many older people, this contradiction is reinforced in dozens of routine interactions with younger people who are better-informed, more competent with technology, and yet impatient and judgmental in ways that proud elders might find distasteful, if not humiliating. Unwilling to expose themselves to the risk of appearing ignorant, older people are apt to withdraw from the conversation, foreclosing even further on the opportunity to learn, and making the cultural barriers separating themselves from the connected digital world even higher.

OATS, both in its training curricula and in its presence in the community, seeks to overcome that with several strategies. One is to create opportunities for older people to get information about technology through trusted channels, in ordinary conversations. This helps them be engaged in discussions and take ownership of the technology as relevant to their own lives and work, rather than simply being a tool for the young. Kamber says it can be as simple as getting people comfortable about the language of technology. "Take collaborative filtering, for example. What does it mean to tell an older adult that there's this thing called collaborative filtering and describe it to them? It demystifies technology just to get people used to the language, so that they realize that when they go on Netflix to choose a movie, that they're getting recommendations based on other people who have chosen similar movies and rated them the same as they have. It's a basic concept that you and I and people in our forties may find natural, but somebody in their sixties and seventies doesn't have a conversation around that."

The other OATS strategy is to create nonthreatening environments where older people can learn. "I think that with older people, there's a reality to asking these questions and to seeming weak, at the business place and in the world, even at the levels that I'm dealing with people, in the nonprofit world," says Kamber. "It suggests to coworkers that maybe they are not as powerful or as knowledgeable as they otherwise are in the workplace. And so for them to learn, there is a real risk."

When dealing with these kinds of situations, Kamber says it's important to create a space where people feel safe taking risks, asking questions, and learning without worrying about being judged or seen as inadequate. Kamber describes the approach as, "I'm sure you know a lot of this stuff already, but it's helpful for people to get retooled on things, and so we're going to start with some of the simple stuff. We respect that you may know some of this, but I just want to give you a chance to ask questions." The key is to create a safe place where they don't feel that they're exposing themselves to business risk or professional risk by engaging in the learning process. That's why instilling patience and a respectful approach to every student is a critical part of the OATS trainer orientation program.

"You feel comfortable here, you're not embarrassed because you don't know," says Lester Johnson, 63, a retired employee of the Federal Reserve Bank who turned to OATS for skills to return to the workforce. "You're around people who are your peers. They understand that we're not all dumb and stupid—there are things we don't know, but we're all eager to learn. The patience is what makes a difference. Like I said, I've been through that. I've been to several classes where if you don't know something, they'll give you one or two of the answers, then you're on your own, and they won't bother. I've known that for *very* real."

NAVIGATING UNMANAGED INFORMATION SPACE

As discussed in Chapter 4, issues of trust and authority related to the generational outlook and established workstyles of Silents and older Boomers can make them initially more skeptical about the value of unmanaged, nonlinear information environments. It is possible that these attitudes underlie some of the resistance observed in older workers to sharing information on public spaces, collaborative content development, transparent relationships, informal communication and knowledge transfer, and other features associated with social computing technologies.

People with experience on the Internet and in connected information environments take for granted many of the quirky, counterintuitive, and potentially dangerous aspects of the experience and have developed tacit skills for dealing with them. Because so much of our understanding of how to navigate in an unmanaged information space arises from trial-and-error and intuition, it can be difficult to recognize and articulate the explicit issues to people who approach information in a more linear way. OATS has discovered that some of these implicit skills come easily to older adults, whereas others require demonstration, reinforcement, and practical application before people with traditional attitudes toward information embrace and use them. However, once those barriers are surmounted, it unlocks a flood of talent and insight that experienced older people can bring to bear in business, community, personal, and social settings.

Validating Information: "One of the things that older adults pick up immediately that is more difficult to teach to younger people is the concept of phishing and false Web sites," says Derr-Daugherty, who has taught technology to various age groups. "When we review the skills they need to learn about how to identify a false e-mail that says it's from Chase Bank or Blockbuster, for instance, they catch on right away." In this case, OATS teaches specific techniques—how to read the status bar, how to check to see if a link actually goes where it says it goes, et cetera. Street smarts do the rest. "They have life experience and wisdom about not being fooled, so all they need to do is translate those skills into reading Web pages and e-mails," Derr-Daugherty continues. "The Web literacy is what we teach them, but they very much bring their own experience and their own common sense to authenticating Web sites and authors and e-mails."

Martinez provides an object lesson in Internet culture with an amusing example. "I show my students the Web site for the tree octopus," she explains with a mischievous smile. "I don't know if you've heard of this Web site. It's called Zapatopi or something like that[3] (see Figure 7.1). And it's a Web site all about the Northwest Pacific tree octopus, which is not a real animal, but they believe it the minute they see it. They're all like, 'Oh, I've never heard of this animal. It's an octopus that climbs trees and it lives in, you know, Seattle or whatever.' At first they don't understand why somebody would go through all the trouble to make up the tree octopus, but then they see that people sometimes just want to have fun with the Web. You can have fun with it. Then they're like, 'This is actually kind of funny,' and

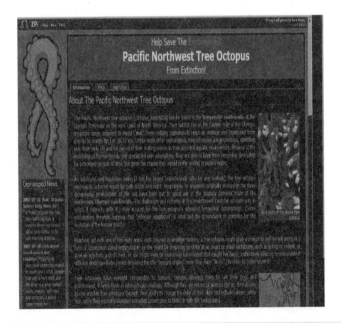

FIGURE 7.1 Don't Believe Everything You See on the Web*

*Source: Zapatopi.net

then they go and start clicking on all the other like stories that are on this site. And I think that they always look for the authority or the serious part of everything and they don't naturally go for the fun right away."

Collective Knowledge: As part of its operations, OATS created a Web site called Senior Planet (http://www .seniorplanet.org—see Figure 2), which includes a shared events calendar, a Wiki-based resource guide for seniors and older workers, and a community of blogs by OATS students, staff, and graduates. The site is maintained by participants in the advanced Internet skills classes, who learn to use Web-based tools for content creation and basic HTML to create links, format pages, and add graphics. Many of the students in the advanced class began with the very basic training program only months before, moving quickly from having no technology skills to speak of to becoming active contributors to a collective knowledge environment. Part of that transition was possible because people were able

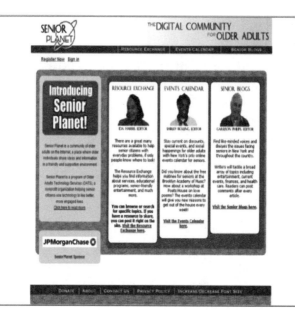

FIGURE 7.2 Senior Planet Homepage*

Source: http://www.seniorplanet.org/home/

to overcome their initial fears and intimidation, and were thus able to pick up the necessary skills quickly in the same way that younger people do, through experimentation. But part of it required OATS to address the specific issues that collaborative content raises for older people.

"It's tough for them," says Martinez. "If they think it's a free-for-all where anybody can come and put up information, they're a little apprehensive. I show them Wikipedia to sort of give them an example of what we're trying to do, and they're very leery of it. They're used to, you know, the *Encyclopedia Britannica* telling me what is true. The first thing that comes out of all their mouths is, 'Well, how do you know if this is true? This isn't true. How do you check the facts?' They're very concerned with that."

Ida Harris is currently enrolled in the advanced Internet class taught by Martinez at the Park Slope YMCA. After retiring as associate director of ambulatory care for one of New York City's largest hospitals, she began taking OATS classes to learn computer skills, and now shares her knowledge and experience from her career in healthcare with others in her community through the resource guide. She had few problems mastering the Wiki tool itself, but it took her some time to get comfortable with the concept behind the technology. "Well, for what I've learned about Wikis, it's a good idea, but you can't believe everything you read on there," she says. "I found out it's just people going in putting down information on their own. Some of the information is factual or some of it may not be, so you need to be careful what you trust. But it has been a great help for me and what I've learned to do." Harris is now managing editor of the Resource Guide and was editing HTML tags in the source code as she conducted this interview.

"I think that explaining the value of collective knowledge, and repeating that value and demonstrating that value is a big contributor to them feeling comfortable and doing the work on the Wiki resource guide," says Derr-Daugherty. "I think a lot of it is a matter of faith right now and that as they start to see more people using it and more exposure of the Web site in media that they're more used to, whatever that may be, other press or print or whatever, that it will come full circle. But regardless, I think that they're very much engaged with the idea of contributing and making a resource that's really valuable and necessary."

Blogging and Social Networking: "At first I thought that the social networking part of the Internet wasn't going to be important to them or that they wouldn't care," says Martinez. "But I've realized with teaching the Senior Planet course that they're really interested in blogging, they're really interested in people hearing their thoughts and sharing their knowledge. They'll write essays for me and they want me to put them on the blog because they want other people to read it. You know, I guess my experience is I didn't think that they had so much passion about taking one step further with technology. Now that I have these students who have gone to two or three of our classes and they're really, really getting into it, they want to share that with other people. I didn't expect that."

Unlike younger people who sometimes seem obsessed with exhibiting themselves through technology like YouTube and MySpace, older people just want to get their experiences out so others can learn from them. "They don't understand MySpace because they feel like there's no end result," observes Martinez. "You know, kids go on, they put their picture up, they tell everybody their life story. Older people aren't interested in that aspect of it. Plus they're afraid of identity theft and things like that. But if there's a goal, like the goal is to create discussion around this, they get really excited and they all have these stories that they've wanted to share, that they wanted to discuss with people, but, you know, their network is limited. So they have an opportunity to get that out there and I think it's a new concept for them.

For most of my students, they're really excited. They don't want to put anything on the resource exchange. They want to blog."

CONNECTING THE GENERATIONS

Another successful aspect of the OATS model is their intergenerational program, where students receive class credit for volunteering as technology tutors for older adults. The program is specifically designed to create connections between the generations on broader issues, using technology as the starting point. "I often joke that technology is just incidental to what we do," says Derr-Daugherty. "The social benefits of the intergenerational program are probably greater than we can measure. We're creating a space where the older adults are comfortable and the younger adults are comfortable and they can create a dialogue with each other. Along the way, they discover that they have things in common."

In the program, one or more youth volunteers are assigned to an OATS class and work one-on-one with the students to provide more personal attention during the workshop sessions. Nia Reyes, 19, heard about the program at her school and started working with OATS after graduating in the spring of 2007. She considers herself about average in terms of technology compared to her peers, but recognizes that that qualifies her as an expert compared to the older people she tutors.

"I pretty much knew what to expect, which was that, you know, they didn't really know how to navigate with the mouse, or little things like that," she says. "But it was just minor problems, because a lot of them caught on to it real quick. They want to do the same things we do on the computer, but they were just never given the opportunity to actually work with these things."

Reyes believes that the experience working with older adults in this setting has increased her own confidence and made her more comfortable interacting with people of all ages when she enters the workforce. She recognizes that technology is going to play a central role in her working life, regardless of whether she opts for a traditional information-work career or pursues her current interests, which include forensics, child care, and cosmetology. Her OATS experience has made her more aware of the technology issues facing older workers and given her skills to be an effective ambassador across the digital age gap.

"What I've found in my personal experience working with young people and seniors is that I think technology might be the only field where seniors just listen to the young people," says Martinez, who is only 26 herself. "Because they don't know that much about technology, and they see kids playing video games and on the computer for hours and hours, they just trust the kids right away. The kids get a big boost out of that. It's like, this person who's 65 or 70 is asking me for help, and it's really surprising how comfortable the two generations just gel completely and form a dialogue through technology that probably is really hard to find anywhere else, you know? Grandkids don't really understand their grandparents, grandparents don't really understand their grandkids, but through technology, because there's a reliance on each other, they completely understand each other. It's really a powerful experience to watch."

KEEPING PACE WITH RAPID CHANGE

For many older workers, the problem is not merely technology but the rapid change that technology represents. Even well-educated and sophisticated people feel the stresses of relentless innovation and wonder how they can keep up. At age 50, Jennifer Pellegrino is at the young end of the demographic served by OATS and no novice when it comes to technology. She currently works as a freelance court reporter, but previously worked in the advertising industry as a media buyer and continues to look for opportunities in that field. Because many agencies are moving from traditional buying methods to online auctions, Pellegrino is concerned about her ability to keep her skills fresh and relevant.

"I'm trying to find out how I can fit the new nontraditional media with the knowledge that I have," she says. "I mean, it's all abuzz out there right now and everybody that I've met so far in the interactive arena is saying, 'Oh, you need to know this to get back in.'" Pellegrino recognizes how new channels like social networks, professional communities of practice, blogs, and other Web 2.0 technologies are both supporting and transforming the way media buyers do their job and is eager to keep pace, but even at a relatively young age, she feels at risk of getting out of the loop. Although she can learn and master digital skills quickly, she recognizes that she lacks the inputs and instincts of the digital generation.

"That's where I think the age thing comes into play," she says, explaining why she has been slow to participate in social networks for career development. "What don't I know that I could be doing, or that I should be doing in order to move along with this group of people at my age and younger? It's not a conflict, but it's something that I'm sensing: *Oops, there's something that I'm missing*, that I need to know in order to progress, maybe not the pace at which they're progressing, but enough to keep my value. My career has already developed, but there's more to continue in order to maintain that career."

Though she took the OATS class to brush up on some office application skills, she finds the confidence-building aspect of the program to be the most valuable. "The most important information I got out of the class is probably to not fear the technology and to move ahead with it," she says. "If there's something that you want to get out of this computer with what we've taught you, you have the power to just go with it. It's not beyond you, no matter what age you are. Don't be afraid of using this new technology just because it's there."

Pellegrino's partner, Beverly Daffner, a retired teacher with three advanced degrees, is slightly older and described herself as hopelessly intimidated by computers before taking the OATS training. She experienced the typical difficulties finding help that was appropriate to her basic level of computer knowledge but nevertheless respected her as an intelligent person.

"There is a bias with people my age, and I think that's from anyone under, I would say, 45 or so," she says. "And I think that still exists and I think that still will exist because I think it's human nature to be more competent than somebody else and then to look down on that person: 'Oh, older people, forget about it, that's a waste, you know, don't bother.'"

For her, the key element of the OATS approach was to demystify the technology so it no longer seemed to represent something hostile and out of reach. The confidence of being able to learn and keep up empowered her to begin contributing to the connected information world at a high level, reflecting her interests and education. "Once we learned about blogging, we went home and developed our own blog," Daffner says. "It was great for me because I just could—I have so many interests and I'm so scattered—I could just free flow."

WHAT OTHER ORGANIZATIONS CAN LEARN FROM OATS

OATS is a community-based nonprofit, operating an intensive program with a small, dedicated staff. Certain aspects of its business model are obviously difficult for organizations with different focuses and objectives to replicate. However, its success in training older adults with virtually no computer skills to become confident, active, and successful contributors to the connected knowledge environment and the workforce contains some useful lessons in overcoming both the cognitive and cultural aspects of the digital age gap. The key lessons are:

- *Technology training for older adults is a specific discipline.* It requires different methods than those that are effective with younger and midcareer workers.

- *It requires a professional approach.* Because of cultural barriers and the lower frustration threshold of older adults, superficial efforts and inconsistent attention to detail dramatically increase the risk of failure.

- *Starting slowly on the basics pays off later.* Older adults who are unfamiliar with technology don't know what they don't know, and are observed to have more difficulty with tasks that younger learners find elementary. Laying a firm foundation enables much more rapid learning later on.

- *Overcoming initial discomfort leads to rapid learning.* If older adults harbor a fear of experimenting with technology, it is harder for them to learn quickly using the trial-and-error methods favored by digital natives. Dispel these fears first to remove a big barrier to learning.

- *Address cultural barriers directly.* These barriers may be in areas of unmanaged information environments that may give older Boomers and Silents difficulty, such as trust and authority in collaborative content development.

- *Create conversations between generations.* These conversations can foster mutual respect and opportunities for reciprocal learning.

- *Older adults will participate fully once they have the skills.* Older people want opportunities to contribute knowledge and are excited by technologies that provide them with a platform.

- *Help older workers manage change.* They want to stay relevant and valuable. Technology competency gives them the confidence to keep their skills fresh in other areas.

OUTCOMES

The success of OATS's model is demonstrated by the continued growth of the organization and by the results of surveys completed by participants at the end of each class or event. More than 80 percent of program respondents ranked the course as "very useful" and described themselves as "very satisfied" with the quality of instruction. Of those looking for work skills, 38 percent considered themselves "much more" prepared to work in a modern information workplace, and all program participants saw some improvement. OATS continues to generate success stories like Vivian Notturno, who recently got a promotion after only six months in her new job, and at age 56, has found new value and opportunity in the information workforce.

ENDNOTES

Most of the material in this chapter is the result of a series of interviews with OATS staff and students, who were extremely generous with their time and insights. The interviews were conducted between May 29–June 5, 2007 at the OATS offices in Park Slope, Brooklyn, and at various training sites around New York City.

1. Older Adults Technology Services, www.oatsny.org
2. Cited in Begley, Sharon. "The Upside of Aging." *Wall Street Journal*, February 16, 2007.
3. "Help Save the Endangered Pacific Northwest Tree Octopus from Extinction!" ZPI Blog, March 9, 2007. http://zapatopi.net/treeoctopus/

~ 8 ~

Ambassadors of the Future: Turning to Younger Workers for Strategic Insights

When Millennials hit the workforce in significant numbers, they are going to shake things up. They are the blue-chip prospects organizations will look to for new energy, new ideas, and titanic productivity. Shelves of books and hundreds of Web sites are full of advice for employers looking to attract, retain, and satisfy them, but Millennials are more than just the next people in the door to fill the places of retiring Boomers. With their numbers, their collective purpose, and their global perspective, they can't help but transform the workplace and the world. Organizations that have the right investments in place to capitalize on the skills and work styles of Millennials will enjoy a significant advantage in recruitment and retention, and will also be best positioned to unleash their vast creative and productive potential.

The main impact of the Millennial generation in the workforce might not be felt for another 10 to 15 years, when the leading edge starts moving up into management roles and the youngest members have completed their educations. Especially with the lead times required to build out

technology infrastructure and modify organizational practices, wouldn't it be nice to have a crystal ball, or at least a
plausible roadmap, to plot out the ways that the Millennials'
agenda will impact the workplace and the marketplace, so
as to be in optimum position to harness their talent?

Sadly, there are no crystal balls—at least none that I
know of. There are, however, various rigorous methodologies for long-term strategic planning that organizations
of all kinds have used to map out opportunities and hedge
against risk. Usually these methods rely on outside consultants, internal teams of experts, or focus groups of existing
customers. Broader-based surveys and polls can point out
trends, but they don't often provide great depth of analysis.
The problem with these approaches is that they exclude or
diminish an important constituency: the people who will
actually make up the future workforce, but currently fall
just short of working age.

Millennials may be objects of study, but they are also,
increasingly, participants in the dialogue, and it is silly (and
rude) for organizations to talk about them as if they are not
already in the room. All young people have an awareness
of their own circumstances beyond what their elders give
them credit for. Connected, self-aware, and sophisticated
Millennials are often particularly perceptive and articulate
when given the opportunity to focus on issues that are important to them. There is little to lose and much to be
gained by seeking out their views, not just as consumers,
but as prospective participants in the knowledge workforce.

This chapter explores one effort to integrate the perspective of future workers into a formal strategic planning
exercise. I offer it as an example because of my familiarity with the issues and the players, and because Microsoft
provided unconditional access to the internal documents
associated with the project. While not every organization
will have the resources or inclination to repeat Microsoft's
experiment in every detail, I think the basic concept of

bringing young people from outside the organization into the planning process has benefits that companies, government agencies, educational institutions, and nongovernment organizations at all levels could profit from.

MICROSOFT AND THE FUTURE OF WORK

Microsoft Corporation, the world's largest software company, has a special interest in determining the possible implications of the arrival of the Millennial generation in the workforce. As a simple matter of competitiveness, maintaining a steady influx of highly skilled programmers and management professionals is absolutely critical to Microsoft's position as an industry leader in the development of valuable intellectual property. Microsoft simply can't afford to lose out in the talent race to companies that offer young people a more attractive work experience.

More broadly, Microsoft plays an enormous role in defining the information technology environment for everyone. Its continued value in the market depends at least in part on accurately anticipating the needs of its customers— the hundreds of millions of people who work with information every day. With product development cycles that can take as long as six or seven years, Microsoft has to guess right about market conditions and business requirements in the work environment nearly a decade in the future as it draws up the specifications for future versions of its core products.

With so much at stake, Microsoft makes enormous investments in market research and engages in extensive dialogues with customers to sound out their impressions and priorities. Research and dialogues are useful, but they necessarily rely solely on the perception of those who are currently in decision-making roles within the organizations—mostly Boomers and GenXers. Likewise, internal visioning exercises within Microsoft reflect the overwhelming preponderance of those cohorts within the present workforce.

In 2004, a group within the Microsoft Business Division (the corporate unit responsible for Microsoft Office and Microsoft Dynamics Business Solutions, among other products) decided that if they wanted to know about the future of the workforce, they would have to ask the future workers themselves. Dan Rasmus, a former analyst with Giga Research (later Forrester Research), had just been hired as Director of Information Work Vision. As a long-time trend watcher and devotee of strategic planning, Rasmus convinced his management to launch a program to bring young people (ages 18 to 23) from around the world together in a structured weeklong exercise around the future of work. He called the initiative the Information Worker Board of the Future.

"The Information Worker Board of the Future was formed in 2004 to take advantage of the perceptions of Millennials, to understand what their capabilities, desires, and expectations are for when they join the workforce," explains Rasmus. "They have not for the most part held down jobs or chosen careers, so we want to understand how the consumer behavior that they have been brought up with as the first generation to really have technology from birth and just be surrounded by it. We want to understand what that means and how it will influence the workforce of the future."

"In my opinion, the reason why they are consulting us is that they have mostly older people in their company and we are younger and not yet 'corrupted' by organizational practices, business hierarchies, and all the corporate politics that come with it," says Varun Sunderraman, a graduate student from India pursuing a master's degree in electrical engineering. "We are still students. We are looking at the world from scratch. We are just rising up. And there may be a chance that we have something interesting to say, and that during conversations we might come up with some good insights into these areas, which will give them ideas into how the emerging workforce would like to deal with their peers and their superiors in their workspace, which is what the future is all about."

The goal of the program was to produce robust visions of the future workplace that Microsoft could use in discussions with customers, and potentially as a basis for long-term product development, recruitment, and human resource planning. The inaugural Board drew 15 students from 10 different countries and convened in the summer of 2004. Upon their arrival at Microsoft's campus in Redmond, Washington, the students were introduced to each other through an exercise that had them explore their past by posting their personal and technological experiences over the last 10 years on long timelines taped to conference room walls. The Board was also asked to forecast events they foresaw over the next 10 years. This exercise was designed from the outset to make sure that the Board members were focused on how their attitudes and thoughts would affect the future.

SCENARIO PLANNING

Following this ice-breaking exercise, the Board was engaged in a traditional scenario planning effort in which they were asked to describe the uncertainties related to the future of work, derive driving forces, and develop a matrix of possible futures.

Scenario planning is a visioning technique for identifying vectors of change and uncertainty, popularized by the Global Business Network (GBN). It involves assembling small groups to identify critical uncertainties in the world ahead, then gaming out how different outcomes to each of the uncertainties might create different worlds with different prevailing conditions. The goal of the exercise is to develop strategies that are robust across as many of the different foreseeable scenarios as possible, so as to minimize the risk of being blindsided by a disruptive change that could occur outside the more limited organization- or industry-wide framework that bounds most strategic planning assumptions.

The process of developing scenarios is an imaginative exercise bounded by reasonable inferences about the possible direction of current trends. It's also fun, which was helpful in keeping the young participants engaged. Figure 8.1 is an illustration prepared by the session facilitators to describe the process.

In the exercise, it's at least as important to consider reasons how and why current trends might *not* continue as we expect them to, as it is to trace them to their logical conclusions. For example, we might think we know something about the direction of energy prices, given the relative likelihood of increases in demand and the high potential for

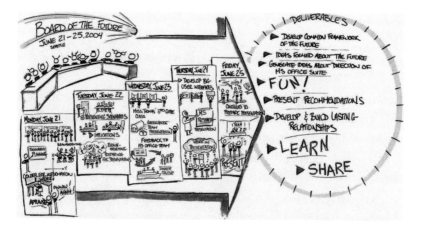

FIGURE 8.1 Board of the Future Agenda

geopolitical turmoil in the primary regions where oil is produced. But what if a new technology like cold fusion suddenly appears and changes the entire model? Outlandish? Unlikely? Perhaps, but if it (or something like it) actually happened, the plans we had made to prepare for one kind of energy market would be completely useless. If we had overcommitted to those plans because we were overconfident in one particular outcome, our entire enterprise would be at risk. It's not necessary for every scenario to include a disruptive element, but it is often helpful to consider at least one set of possibilities where something upsets the applecart.

That's why it is important to have a diversity of views within the planning group. It might seem like a good idea to include a lot of experts, but in reality, too much expertise, specialization, or homogeneity within the group can limit the field of inquiry, and may potentially omit an important factor from consideration simply because it is outside the experience of the participants. Who, in a group of oil company executives, geologists, and international affairs experts, would be willing to throw out the possibility of a cheap alternative energy source appearing overnight? That's the kind of idea that might occur to an idealistic young college student with no vested interest in the outcome, not an *expert* with a reputation to defend.

Diversity of national origin, educational background, economic status, and age can also be helpful. A group composed entirely of Americans can't be expected to consider factors that might occur instantly to someone from India or Brazil. A group of affluent, educated software developers, despite their best efforts, would likely impose their own values and priorities on any discussion involving technology. And a group made up entirely of Boomers and GenXers would naturally project their own generational experience ahead into the future, possibly also influenced by contemporaneous cultural inputs such as science fiction and films, which shaped their early ideas of how the future should look (in Microsoft's internal exercise, one of the future scenarios began to sound a lot like the 1980s sci-fi film *Road Warrior*).

In Microsoft's case, the question was how to design information software for the future workplace that has value to customers even if global conditions or organizations change in significant ways. What capabilities would future workers find important? How would emerging conditions influence the implementation of different technologies? What should the company look for as warning signals indicating critical changes to the underlying environment that might impact its strategic efforts?

It was an easy decision to reach out to younger people through the Board of the Future program, as the impact of Millennials on the workforce was one of the critical uncertainties surrounding these questions. The viewpoints of those about to take their first steps into the workplace were not only valuable as an outside perspective, but directly germane to the question at hand.

The first step in any scenario planning process is to identify which dynamics in the global environment are actually uncertain, and which of those uncertainties is most critical in defining the conditions of the different scenarios. The members of the Board of the Future 2004 generated 85 uncertainties, then voted to select the ones that were most important and most uncertain in response to the focal question of the future of information work. Each uncertainty was given a set of polarities to further define it. Combinations of polarities were tested to see which intersections provided the most divergent and challenging scenarios.

Microsoft later ran an exercise with an internal team from the Information Worker division and then again as a participant in a cross-industry GBN-hosted forum on developing and using scenarios held in 2004. One of the more interesting outcomes of the Board of the Future program was the opportunity to compare the priorities and issues raised by Millennials to those raised by the other groups dominated by older generations. Figure 8.2 maps out the differences and commonalities across the groups.

The top three priorities for Millennials—education, the digital divide, and basic information work literacy—reflect three core generational values: the connection between knowledge and success, commitment to broad-based social justice and empowerment, and the need for pervasive collaboration and information access as precursors to other fields of activity. Cherie Wilson, a recent graduate of the University of Pennsylvania, articulated a common theme from the group: "We have a huge digital divide in addition to an income gap and disparities in education, and I think that's something that needs to be presented here, especially since technology and education are so closely linked. We need to make technology more accessible."

Eventually, the Board defined their uncertainties as the organization of work (managed and hierarchical or distributed/individualistic) and the stability of the world (turbulent and conflicted, or normalizing and stable). The intersection of these uncertainties creates a grid with four quadrants, each corresponding to a combination of possible outcomes. The quadrants become the scenarios, and are given names that define their essential characters. Figure 8.3 illustrates the configuration and characteristics of the scenarios that the Board adopted.

FOLLOWING UP: BOARD OF THE FUTURE 2005

What became clear from the first Board of the Future was the need for follow-on work. The following year, Microsoft recruited another group of young people and continued

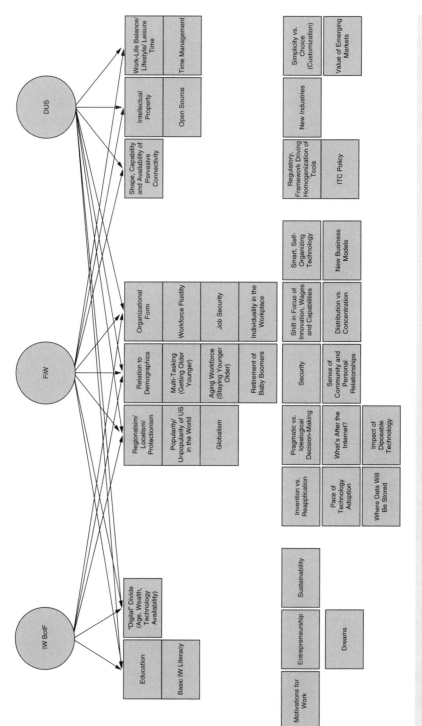

FIGURE 8.2 Issues Raised by Different Scenario Planning Groups

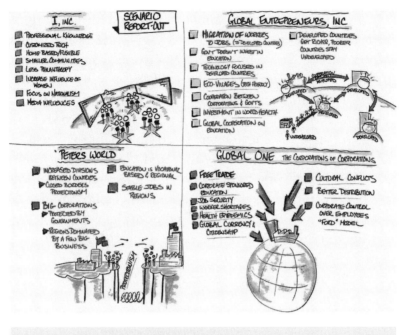

FIGURE 8.3 Board of the Future Scenarios

the dialogue about the future. Twelve undergraduate and graduate college students from India, China, Russia, Israel, Saudi Arabia, Hungary, Sweden, Brazil, Spain, and the United States were selected from an applicant pool of about 175 candidates. Their fields of study varied from international relations, linguistics, anthropology, and business to more technical disciplines such as engineering and computer science. Sessions took place over the course of a week in August 2005, in Budapest, Hungary.

To make effective use of time and drive toward meaningful results, the Microsoft team and the students focused on two central issues:

- What were the attitudes of the Millennials toward work and the underlying drivers for those attitudes?
- How could education better prepare students for the workplace?

The young Board members produced three outputs from the week of exercises. First, they were asked to interpret survey data gathered by Microsoft from applicants for spots on the Board of the Future 2005, as well as the 2004 Board members and candidates. Next, they were exposed to scenario planning methods and were asked to extend narratives and create characters to complement the versions generated by Microsoft's Boomer and GenX-heavy internal teams. Finally, they used both the interpretation of the survey data and the scenarios to offer a forecast of the workplace in 2015 from the point of view of the average information worker. All of the outputs fed into Microsoft's own strategic planning processes, and were made available both internally and externally as part of the ongoing dialogue with customers.

TECHNOLOGY AND SOCIETY: THE PERCEPTION STUDY

Preliminary to the Budapest sessions, Microsoft created and distributed a survey of perceptions about a range of future work and life issues to all applicants, as well as applicants and Board members from 2004. Questions in the survey focused on the following issues:

- Impact of demographics on the future workforce
- Extent and nature of IT penetration into job roles and tasks
- Changes to education practices and the education system
- Impact of new technologies on the structure of organizations
- Implications of technology on community and communications

- Implications of global connectedness and technology on creativity and language

During the Board sessions, the students were broken up into three groups to analyze the results from the perspective of individuals, society, and technology providers. They were then asked to create recommendations based on the data. The idea was to get students thinking about their own attitudes, as well as apply their analytical skills to provide greater depth to survey data.

The recommendations from the perspective of individuals tended to reinforce other data regarding the priorities of Millennials: they value work/life balance and will seek out employers who use technology in creative ways to smoothly integrate the two.

The recommendations of the workgroup on social implications emphasized the role of government and nongovernmental organizations (NGOs) in providing ubiquitous access to connectivity across economic and demographic divides. They also pointed to the "need to reassure people about technology's positive role . . . [and] market to overcome fear of IT's impact on society." They recommended that technology be integrated into education as a language skill: "part of the toolset of learning, not a thing itself to be learned." The Board also issued some strong guidance to technology suppliers (such as Microsoft), mostly related to simplification of the information environment, the interface, and devices.

In the education integration sessions, the students shared their overview of education systems from their home countries, with Microsoft and HP representatives adding additional information for some countries not represented by students. The students then filled out a timeline that created a discussion context. This timeline represented their initial encounters with various technologies in both their personal and educational lives. In most cases, technology was being taught in isolation (e.g., computer skills) rather than being integrated as an enabler of learning, research, and personal expression within the context of traditional education subject matter. Students were learning how to use the features of PowerPoint as a technical skill, but not how to create a persuasive presentation as a communication skill, or to use software as a way to present a history research project or a biology lab report.

As might be expected, the students spoke with quite a bit of authority on the subject of education. They clearly recognized the necessity of knowledge skills as the cost of entry into the new global economy and are anxious to see both public and private institutions make the investments to ensure the broadest distribution of those skills. Based on their experiences, they recommended the following:

- *Student-centered curriculum.* Recognizing that the traditional taxonomy of educational subjects is blending and transforming more quickly than the system can adapt, this approach allows students to take initiative over their own education by defining their own fields of study.

- *Problem-based learning.* Solves the problem of technology compartmentalization in education by requiring students to come up with solutions using technological innovations and resources.

- *Teach the Web.* Rather than fearing the consequences of exposing students to the Internet, educators should teach good practices, knowledge hygiene, and boundaries so students can use networks openly and responsibly, without external restriction.

- *Content sharing among teachers.* Build networks of students and teachers so teachers can learn and share new practices and keep up with the pace of innovation.

Across all of the groups and discussions, the Board members were extremely sensitive to the issues of technology complexity and the problems this causes to society, organizations, and individuals because access to information is now so essential. Michael Maturo, a recent graduate of the University of Southern California in computer science and business administration, put it this way: "I think point blank, technology needs to be more intuitive and more social. Instead of society needing to become more technology-based, we need to have technology come to us. The problem we're seeing is that people like my parents, who are not very old, and my grandparents, they don't have an intuitive sense of technology—and that gap is only looking to increase. So we need to find a way to close that gap. When I'm 50 years old, I want to be able to learn the latest technology and keep up with it. Judging from what I've seen, with clients I've done consulting for, trying to teach older workers to use computers is extremely difficult. And it's really because it's a way of thinking."

"Technology may help bridge the gap between work and life," says Sofya Mezhorina, a linguistics and education student at Tambov State University in Russia. "It can create the world-class business. When appropriately used, it may help to reduce the amount of work to be done, it may help to prioritize, utilize, and organize tasks and do them better so people have more time to spend with their family and other personal needs. But if we talk about the social sphere, the most important thing is making technology more user-friendly and more convenient. It should be simpler, more accessible, more affordable. It should be very easy to use, for anyone."

REFINING THE SCENARIOS: CHARACTERS AND NARRATIVES

The second Board of the Future also engaged in the scenario planning process, but did not start from scratch the way the first Board did. Because the field of inquiry was more limited, the group began by adopting Microsoft's internal scenarios, illustrated in Figure 8.4. In this model, the critical uncertainties are the future prospects of globalization (increasing global integration, or retrenchment back to national and regional alignments?) and the dominant model for organizations (centralized hierarchies, or distributed networks?)—similar to the perceptions of the first Board of the Future, but oriented slightly differently.

Once the initial conditions of the different scenarios were defined, the group worked to flesh out the details of each world. Part of that process involved creating typical characters—students, workers, citizens—and exploring the facets of their day-to-day lives under the global conditions of their particular scenario. The facilitator led the discussion to draw out very specific differences between the

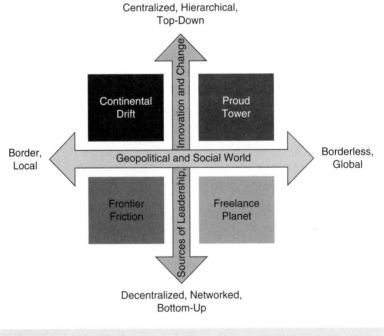

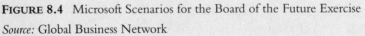

FIGURE 8.4 Microsoft Scenarios for the Board of the Future Exercise
Source: Global Business Network

worlds around issues of importance to Microsoft's core interests. Questions posed by the moderator and the group zeroed in on the ways that technology would support different aspects of work and life. For example, how might concepts of privacy and transparency differ in a world of centralized corporate control versus one of dynamic, bottom-up networks? And how are those differences reflected in the experiences of ordinary people with their workplace technology?

The scenario stories created by the Board provided some interesting answers to those questions. What came through, in addition to the participants' personal experiences in education and in diverse cultural settings, was a palpable distaste for the scenarios involving the bordered world and hierarchically organized organizations. It was obviously uncomfortable for these globally minded students to visualize scenarios where technology was used to prevent the sharing of knowledge or to enforce orthodoxy. Their vision of corporate hegemony is an Orwellian nightmare; their vision of a retreat away from global culture to one of national and regional particularism echoes with loss and loneliness. These are not worlds that the workers of the future want to live in, and they see the consequences of choices that lead to those scenarios as far more grave than their older colleagues.

FORECASTS

While the scenario development process is fascinating, the high-value outputs for the sponsoring organization are the concrete forecasts and recommendations that come from "wind-tunneling" various ideas through the scenario framework to test their resilience. The final phase of the Board's work consisted of boiling down the different discussions into a vision for the future of the information workplace in 2015, based on their assessment of the likely vectors of various dynamics such as technological innovation, demographic change, economic forces, and government policy. These were the Board's conclusions:

1. *"Work anyplace, anytime" finally becomes seamless and easy*—and firms encourage or at least allow it while people (employees and freelancers) provide their own tools. These capabilities trickle down to consumer and home technologies (accessible everywhere, etc.). This includes working with more people anywhere on the globe without having to travel, using rich technology like shared spaces, voice over IP, and desktop videoconferencing.

2. *The user experience of technology becomes integrated*, adaptive, natural, contextually intelligent, seamless, and just plain better.

3. *Novel methods of visualization and automatic translation enhance the experience of working with abstract and complex data.* The number of documents produced will be dramatically reduced. It will not be necessary to explain or summarize data, because that will be handled by the visualization tools.

4. *Technology at home converges* to include all forms of entertainment. Technology's reach extends into clothing and housewares, and personal finance ties to the shopping experience. Consumer technology (and content) pours into the workplace.

5. *Learning will be driven by the individual, will be delivered on-demand, and will be continuously available.* Learning will span peers, experts and communities as sources, both formally and informally. Learning will be a lifelong experience.

Another interesting output of the group was the creation of a hypothetical new device to solve the problems of access and complexity. The Board called this device the "red phone," in homage to the hotline telephones that connected the U.S. President and the Soviet Premier in the days of the Cold War. The original red phone was a model of simplicity: just pick up the handset and the other party would answer. This had a certain logic, in that the hotline system was designed to avert misunderstandings over the launch of nuclear missiles—certainly not a situation where you would want technology to get in the way of human interaction.

The red phone device designed by the Board echoed that approach. It provides all-purpose access to the entire underlying information ecosystem: documents, media content, people (e.g., via voice, instant message, e-mail), different networks and systems, and complex datasets, but does so through a simplified interface that dispenses with the complicating metaphors of file hierarchies, passwords, URLs, network addresses, and overlapping software applications. People (and presumably organizations) can customize the interface to their specific needs or to the local language and conditions. "The red phone device would provide universal access through an individualized interface," explains Cherie Wilson. "You could customize by region, by age group, by whatever task you were trying to do at the moment. It's something that everyone would have access to—but at the same time, the individual still knows what's going on, and it's specific to that person. Whether you're a student in a remote country in Africa or a trader at Goldman Sachs, you'd still have access to this technology—it's just a different interface."

Issues of simplicity and accessible design were very much on the minds of the group. Michael Maturo, the electrical engineering student, recognizes the role of software designers and vendors in the process and is optimistic about the growing awareness of the importance of people-centric design within both the commercial and academic arms of the technology industry. "The curriculum for Java programming and software usually includes very technical concepts. You have arrays and types of matrices and math problems. But one of the things that we're introducing now—we're introducing at USC—is user interface design. So now we're getting the people who have the technical skills and the programming technology background and we're teaching them how to be more social programmers. That's the first step toward actually getting the people who are experts to think in that realm. Because they're not doing it now. You usually have a separate set of people who tweak user interfaces. But if we start thinking on a more fundamental technical level to make user interface design really important, that's the sea change. The sea change is how you design software and hardware from the ground up. That I think is the difference."

OUTCOMES

The Board of the Future program was helpful to Microsoft in several ways. First and most obviously, it infused the company's internal strategic planning process with new perspectives that helped validate some of its own conclusions and caused reassessment of others. The Board's input into the scenario storylines was incorporated into the official scenarios that the vision and leadership team uses as the basis for its future vision whitepapers, makes available to the rest of the company for planning purposes, and shares with customers in strategic-level executive briefing sessions. Some of the material contributed by the Board found its way into the New World of Work vision articulated by Microsoft Chairman Bill Gates in 2005, and into the People-Ready Business positioning that the company adopted in 2006.

The Board of the Future also garnered favorable media coverage from press and analysts, helping to burnish Microsoft's thought-leadership credentials. According to Microsoft's internal metrics, broadcast coverage of the program reached an audience of more than 37 million people worldwide in 2005. Many of the participants went on to appear on local television programs and gave interviews about their experiences to local media when they returned to their host countries. The members of the Board also became informal ambassadors of both the Board of the Future project and Microsoft. Several remain part of the Information Work Vision and Leadership extended network of opinion leaders.

Millennials and succeeding generations have a lot to tell us about the shape of the world to come. Of course, organizations conduct polling and focus groups among youth all the time, largely dedicated to determining their preferences as consumers. Exercises such as the Board of the Future are meant to assess the potential of the next generation as *producers and contributors*, through a formal process that gives full weight to their insights. This is not a conversation *about* Millennials as if they were objects to be studied under a microscope—it's a conversation *with* Millennials that recognizes the validity of their perspectives and priorities as drivers of change, as citizens and workers as well as consumers.

In other words, the organizational commitment to engage with Millennials as partners in the formation of a strategic vision can be as valuable as the direct knowledge gained from the engagement. Strategic planning is a crucial discipline for organizations operating in an uncertain world. When it is a closed process, conducted by experts and senior people (who inevitably bring their generational biases with them), it runs a greater risk of missing emergent trends or misjudging the potential for discontinuities that could disrupt the entire global environment. Opening up the planning process to younger perspectives as a matter of course rather than novelty hedges against the risks of generational myopia and also sends a strong positive signal to members of the rising generation.

~9~

Across the Digital Age Gap

The first five chapters of this book examined the issues that may contribute to the digital age gap across society and within organizations, with an emphasis on the specific challenges of increasing technological complexity and generational differences in outlook. The next section looked at two efforts to narrow the gap by increasing intergenerational dialogue and understanding. This final chapter discusses how organizations can develop practices and deploy technology to attract, motivate, and empower workers of all ages.

Many of the analysts and industry experts I interviewed for this book agreed on one point: people will adopt technology when they perceive it to be easy and helpful. Generational differences come into play in defining what "easy" and "helpful" mean, beyond the obvious, universal goals of completing work faster, spending less time on low-value tasks, being recognized for accomplishments, and having some scheduling flexibility. Different generations in the workplace not only do things differently, but have different things they want to get done. Silents want to maximize economic value, strengthen institutions, and forge a consensus. Boomers want to self-actualize, act on their ideals, and produce visible accomplishments. GenXers want to get more done in less time, make processes work better, and be left alone. Millennials want to do socially meaningful work, collaborate, multitask, participate, and receive feedback. Members of those generations naturally gravitate to the tools that best suit their values and priorities, and resist those they see as adding complexity without commensurate reward.

The digital age gap arises from a conflict between people and technology: their expectations, their experiences, their priorities, and their ways of understanding work and the world. It's not the only barrier to the productive application of new technology in the workplace, but it is an aggravating and complicating factor that is poorly understood and rarely addressed. Organizations looking to effectively manage across the digital age gap in an increasingly sophisticated connected information workplace should ask themselves five questions:

1. Are you clearly explaining the benefits of technology?
2. Are you providing a business context for your technology policies?
3. Are you making technology accessible to different workstyles?
4. Does your organizational culture support your technology strategy?
5. Are you building bridges instead of walls?

ARE YOU CLEARLY EXPLAINING THE BENEFITS OF TECHNOLOGY?

Because technology is so present in contemporary culture and society, few people can avoid forming opinions about the latest tech trends and gadgets based on media reports, marketing and advertising, limited personal experience, or anecdotal evidence. As we've seen, older people may be apt to perceive blogs as undisciplined, wikis as unreliable, and collaborative content as a threat to institutional authority. Boomers puzzle over Millennials who prefer text messaging to face-to-face contact. Some GenXers disdain social networks as shallow and a waste of time, or rage against volumes of pointless, random e-mail generated by Boomers jostling for attention. Millennials dismiss structured e-learning and deep content as boring and tediously linear, and e-mail as slow and unresponsive compared to the immediacy of IM.

These attitudes arise because people have experienced the relevant technology in a limited context. No one has taken the time to demonstrate the applicability of the particular tools to their requirements, or demonstrated the fuller potential of a tool to solve a problem specific to their job role. As we saw in Chapter 7, older people rapidly overcame their anxiety and skepticism about collaborative content once they saw they were able to collaborate on content *relevant to their interests*. They not only embraced the concept of wikis, but also mastered the fairly advanced skills necessary to create new links and topics despite their entire lack of prior familiarity with the technology. People's direct experience of concrete benefits quickly outweighed their abstract doubts and motivated them to surmount a formidable barrier to entry.

This same approach can be effective in dispelling the other myths and stereotypes surrounding technology, whether they arise from generational attitudes or other sources. This is not simply a matter of training people how to use the features of a particular application in general, but going the extra step of showing how the new tool or practice snaps into an existing task and makes it simpler, faster, or more convenient *for that particular worker, not just for the organization or people in general*.

For example:

- Show people how to use blogs to communicate informal knowledge about practices directly relevant to their jobs. Perhaps provide humorous examples of dos and don'ts to model appropriate behavior.

- Create a directory of RSS feeds and podcasts, organized around topics, people, departments, and disciplines, then show people how to subscribe to the content that interests them from within their familiar work environment (e.g., e-mail application, browser, personal workspace).

- Create scenarios, stories, and concrete examples that help people understand when it is best to use various modes of communication (IM, e-mail, phone, in-person) and what behavior is appropriate to each mode. Written style guides may be helpful for workers who prefer to learn from documentation rather than experimentation.

- Demonstrate how to set up and provision a shared workspace around a project that the user(s) will find familiar and relevant, and show them where to find the design elements and web parts that can make their site fun, distinctive, and tailored to their personal or team needs.

- Provide guidance on how to simplify the information application environment, so that people can get the most useful set of capabilities from the fewest number of applications. Try to discourage individuals and departments from adopting "point solutions" (applications that only do one thing, or have interface behavior that is inconsistent with the rest of the user's environment).

Many organizations make the mistake of assuming that if they simply make a technology tool available and explain the features, people will use it—and use it productively and appropriately. That's an especially easy assumption for GenX managers because that is how they are accustomed to adopting new technology themselves: without much external direction or explicit guidance. The connections between features and benefits seem obvious to them—perhaps because the products were designed and marketed by people with a similar outlook toward technology—but may need further elaboration to people who lack the knowledge or life experience to draw correct inferences from clues provided by the vendor or implementer.

A lot of generational misunderstandings about technology arise because people with less intuitive familiarity with certain applications initially have difficulty recognizing that it's okay *not* to use every function just because it's there. Everyone has received email or documents from people who just discovered how to change fonts, add colors, or incorporate other unfortunate or inappropriate elements into the design. This syndrome has the potential to get far more prevalent as richer visualization and multimedia tools get integrated into the mainstream information work environment, and routine documents have to "scream" to get the attention of their audience. Most people eventually figure out the rules of information etiquette for themselves, but organizations could spare their people some time and potential embarrassment by making good (and bad) practices explicit. Keep in mind that the learning styles of older workers favor linear, rule-based instruction over trial-and-error. Tip sheets, step-by-step instructions, and style guide documents can save your older workers a lot of stress and grief.

Members of the technoliterate generations may also assume that confused users will raise questions or challenge aspects of the technology that aren't working well so that the problems can be fixed. After all, that's how they express their opinions—bluntly, on blogs and through other channels, with the confidence that they are asking pertinent questions and raising reasonable objections. But as we have seen, older workers—particularly powerful, experienced, and knowledgeable older workers—are not as eager to participate in these conversations for a variety of good reasons. It can be a big mistake for technology strategists to take end-user silence as consent, as problems with implementation and uptake may only become obvious much later. Reach out and follow up with users, and create non-threatening ways for less confident or tech-savvy users of all ages to express their concerns.

It may also not be enough to expect early adopters and evangelists to do the legwork. Consultant and author Dave Pollard observes, "I'd always expected that the younger and more tech-savvy people in any organization would be able to show (not tell) the older and more tech-wary people how to use new tools easily and effectively. But in thirty years in business, I've almost never seen this happen. Millennials will use IM, blogs, and personal Web pages (internal or on public sites like LinkedIn, MySpace, and FaceBook) whether they're officially sanctioned or not, but they won't be evangelists for these tools."[1]

Overburdened IT departments may object that it is unfeasible to provide such a detailed amount of support and customized training. Perhaps, but there is an unavoidable trade-off between the productive capabilities of sophisticated connected information applications and the complexities they create for ordinary people in the workplace. You can't make the problem go away just because a tool seems simple enough to an IT professional that it shouldn't really require much training or acculturation.

No organization wants, or can afford, to see a multimillion-dollar technology initiative fail for want of the final, necessary step of connecting the technology to users. Creating good practices around the use of new dynamic knowledge technology should be part of the calculated upfront costs, along with licensing, integration, deployment, and technical support. Training should take generational factors into account and be delivered in formats appropriate to the learning styles of different users. Organizations that do not have the resources to support this project internally should look to outside resources or partners with industry- and role-specific experience. In some cases, reciprocal men- toring between younger and older workers—discussed later in this chapter—could provide a cost-effective solution with other benefits to the organization.

Bottom line: People will expend far more effort in pur- suit of tangible benefits. An upfront investment in demon- strating the concrete application of a new tool or technology is likely to pay off in substantially greater uptake down the line.

ARE YOU PROVIDING A BUSINESS CONTEXT FOR YOUR TECHNOLOGY POLICIES?

There's a good reason (beyond catchiness) that some people refer to Millennials as Generation Why. Inquisitive, entitled, and brimming with self-esteem, the most junior members of the workforce do not accept policies at face value and give trust only when it has been earned. They also have considerably more knowledge and experience with tech- nology than they do with other aspects of the working world. Whereas a more senior worker may know where to find a document, whom to contact to resolve a problem, or what to do in a particular situation, the younger person has to look it up—and the way they know how to do that is through computer-based search and collaboration. If an organization doesn't have enterprise search, or a document repository, or an expertise location system, or internal blogs and communities where people share knowledge, younger workers may reasonably look for some outside solution to fill that gap so they can do their jobs. They may also simply not recognize the same boundaries between personal and professional life as older people because their life experience has been so extensively mediated by technology, and those boundaries mean less to them.

Younger workers are looking to contribute, demonstrate value, and build job skills using the tools and methods they are familiar with. Those personal priorities can seem more present to the worker than abstract, seemingly arbitrary policies governing the use of technology in the workplace. That's why it is important to provide people with a business context for technology decisions that affect their personal work environments, even if the rationales for those decisions are not "need to know" information for lower-level employees.

This is true in general, but especially critical when it comes to GenXers and Millennials. Younger people will almost certainly resist management and IT efforts to restrict what they see as natural sharing of information if those efforts are perceived as arbitrary, or emanating from the boss's desire to retain personal power by controlling the flow of information. However, they can grasp the financial impact of liability arising from compliance problems or the potential risks of confidential IP falling into the wrong hands—*if* someone takes the time to point those things out in a credible, respectful way.

Organizations looking to employ a lot of younger workers should get used to the idea of having fuller conversations about the business context for their technology policies. Some useful areas of discussion might include:

- *Detailed descriptions of what kinds of content can be shared with whom,* and the reasons why it is necessary to be discrete with certain information (e.g., "we could be sued" or "we don't want our competitors finding out about this").

- *Information retention and privacy practices, written in clear language, not eye-glazing, boiler-plate legalese.* People will have a better sense of boundaries about the style and content of their communications if they have a realistic expectation of when to consider them potentially public rather than private.

- *Appropriate forms of expression in different media.* For example, abbreviations that may be useful in short text messages should not be used in e-mail. Off-the-cuff observations and informal remarks are great for adding a personal voice to internal blogs and discussion threads, but send the wrong messages to customers on externally facing sites.

- *What applications can and cannot be installed on work computers*, and why (e.g., "video sharing uses too much bandwidth and slows down the network for everyone" or "this Web-based application is known to include Adware that can mess up your system").

- *Challenges in implementing popular capabilities* (e.g., instant messaging), giving reasons, proposing workarounds if possible, possibly even soliciting suggestions from users.

- *Clear policies* for resolution of these issues if there is a problem.

To experienced leaders in the organization, the reasons behind technology policies may seem self-evident (along with the reason for obeying them: *because you work here and we pay you!*), but it would be a mistake for organizations to automatically assume that workers in nonmanagement roles or with shallow commitments to the organization will make the connection between their personal work habits and the fortunes of their employers if management does not take the time to share that information.

Younger people raised in an immediate, globally connected, and self-aware world have a sophisticated understanding of strategic realities; they will also appreciate being included in the larger conversation. As we saw in Chapter 8, organizations can tap the unique insights and experiences of the next generation to inform all manner of strategic decisions and work through the uncertain implications of technological change. If motivating and retaining young employees is an organizational goal, then it is worth taking the time to find and honestly express the common interest that organizations and employees have in adopting certain practices or using (or not using) various kinds of technology at work.

ARE YOU MAKING THE TECHNOLOGY ACCESSIBLE TO DIFFERENT WORKSTYLES?

We have been assuming that changes to information work technology require changes to personal practices and work-style, because up until recently, that has mostly been true. When a new software application or device is introduced into an existing practice, the people doing that job need to learn how to use it—not just from a feature/function perspective, but also to increase their overall productivity, efficiency, or quality of output in the context of their work. Otherwise, why bother?

Connected information work technology poses a particular challenge because it is intended to be used by people in non-technical jobs, but sometimes demands expert-level skills to use effectively. Unlike the software developers who designed the product and view each added feature as a benefit (and an achievement), ordinary workers make their own personal determinations about how much software expertise is enough to do their job, and how much constitutes a burden and a bother. They cannot be expected to embrace each new capability just because it is there; indeed, even well-meaning changes to familiar products can breed resentment and resistance.

Additionally, most current information work applications are collaborative and distributed, and so require a critical mass of users before they become useful to any one individual. The deployment of this kind of technology can come to resemble a classic game theory problem of collective action. If social software is disruptive, difficult to learn, and not useful until enough people have learned it in any case, then there is a good, rational reason to wait and see if the deployment is going to be successful before investing one's own effort into learning the new tool. After all, what's the point of being the only person using a shared calendar, or the only contributor to a knowledge base? Of course, if enough people adopt the wait-and-see approach, you don't get critical mass and the promised benefits don't materialize, leading to abandonment of the strategy. The early adopters are punished for their enthusiasm, and the laggards are rewarded for their skepticism—precisely the wrong outcome and the wrong lessons.

The best way out of this dilemma is to make the barriers to entry as low as possible. That way, individuals do not have to risk as much by disrupting tried-and-true practices or investing valuable time (and patience and prestige) learning a new skill that might turn out to be a dead-end anyway. As we have seen, however, the definition of "low barriers" varies according to technological sophistication and generational outlook. What is child's play for a Millennial may be beyond the frustration threshold of an older Boomer; what seems pleasingly straightforward to a less tech-savvy user may drive a GenXer crazy because it lacks a fine-grained level of user control or dispenses with a familiar metaphor.

Fortunately, a lot of applications that support social computing and collaboration are much more flexible than earlier types of software. Some new technologies offer much lower barriers to entry because the software is converging with the way people actually work, rather than forcing people to think more like computers in order to do their jobs. The following design principles may help organizations reduce the friction associated with the introduction of new technology by making it less disruptive for workers.

Use customization to reduce the complexity of the digital environment. System integrators, IT staff, or users can preset environmental defaults within software applications to reduce the end user's experience of change and disruption and make the new software look and act like familiar tools, both digital and analog. Complicated features can be stripped out and disabled. Templates can be built and deployed to make new digital tools (such as forms) look and feel more like their real-world counterparts. Updated versions of software can be configured to resemble previous versions until users are comfortable with the new capabilities.

Enable alternative input methods. As we have seen, the mouse and keyboard sometimes pose a barrier to those without extensive familiarity with computers, to anyone who has never learned to type, or to people in jobs where it is not convenient to enter data with both hands. It's a safe bet that many senior managers keep their reports and communications terse because it takes too long to compose their thoughts on the keyboard. Brevity can be a virtue, but not when organizations are scrambling to capture the subtle, specific, and tacit knowledge of their most experienced people before they retire.

Alternative forms of input such as TabletPCs and PDAs allow people to write in longhand and convert their writing to digital form with increasing precision, or add handwritten comments in the margins of digital documents. Speech recognition and voice-to-text are becoming more accurate as pattern recognition algorithms enable the computer to learn people's accents and speech patterns. Digital audio and video are now easily captured on devices as portable as mobile phones. Clips can be transferred to a database, tagged and indexed for later search and retrieval, posted on blogs, or disseminated through Podcasts.

Alternative inputs are already coming into wider use in industry applications such as healthcare (TabletPCs and PDAs are much more practical replacements for traditional clipboards in clinical settings than mice and keyboards), retail (pen-based portable devices and barcode scanners for inventory and line-buster mobile checkout), film and video production (motion capture suits and sensors), and others, and the range of options is expanding all the time. Giving users an alternative to the mouse and keyboard can be a very simple way to lower a simple but salient barrier to more general collaboration and knowledge capture activities within an organization.

Use familiar methods to do new things. Even when the underlying concept behind a new knowledge practice is not especially threatening, the extra steps required to actually employ the practice day-to-day can be enough of a barrier to discourage beleaguered users from integrating it into their work routines. Take the example of the faculty committee from Chapter 1: the e-mail listserve they employed, although inefficient, was familiar and within their comfort zone, while the threat of change to a new platform activated all kinds of latent resistance. The professors didn't want to go to a new workspace, have to adapt to an unfamiliar interface, and risk pressing the wrong buttons.

But what if the collaborative resources of the workspace were accessible within the familiar application environment of the e-mail client? What if they could have published to the discussion group or the group blog by e-mailing their post to the site address (using the exact same method in which they responded to group e-mails), or started a meeting or real-time discussion from their e-mail contact list? What if the "Save as" default on their word processors pointed to a shared site instead of their individual hard drives, and document routing workflow was embedded in the document creation environment (e.g., the word processing application), rather than requiring a separate step to save and e-mail to the group?

All of these steps represent much smaller, less obvious modifications to the work process that the participants were already comfortable with, as opposed to the disruptive migration to an entirely new hosted environment. The risks to the participants (i.e., fear of appearing incompetent, concerns over the transparency of the new process, inability to exert their influence over the process in familiar ways) are much reduced, and the chances of the people actually gaining the benefits of an improved knowledge process are greatly increased.

The capabilities to support communication, collaboration, data access, and workflow within the existing knowledge work environment are already present in the current versions of business productivity applications and servers. That is, organizations can make these capabilities available to the broad base of information workers without deploying new infrastructure or making disruptive changes to the end-user environment. No deployment is painless, but organizations should consider the benefits of gradually exposing new collaborative capabilities in the context of familiar, well-used, and well-supported applications rather than experimenting with a growing assortment of specialized "best of breed" solutions that can complicate the lives of information workers and IT administrators alike.

Make knowledge tools ubiquitous. It can be difficult to know in advance which knowledge applications will prove popular and which will not. Even pilot tests may not reveal the full range of responses that a given technology will unleash when ordinary workers start experimenting with ways to use it in the contexts of their jobs and roles. While it may be tempting for cost, management, and cultural reasons to restrict certain tools to bleeding-edge environments or power users, the full benefits of collaboration and knowledge sharing are maximized when they are extended across the length and breadth of the enterprise (and sometimes even beyond, to partners and customers).

If you have made an organizational commitment to personal and team Web spaces, or voice over IP, or instant messaging, or any of the other transformative knowledge technologies and their accompanying practices, go all out. If the tools work, they work. People will start using them, discovering benefits unforeseen by even the most strategic IT planners, and the resulting cultural shift will spur universal adoption.

DOES YOUR ORGANIZATIONAL CULTURE SUPPORT YOUR TECHNOLOGY STRATEGY?

Culture is the critical factor in the success of any organizational initiative, technological or otherwise. Organizations perceive themselves as innovative or conservative, disciplined or informal, social or individualistic. Changes that go against the grain of the culture, regardless of their logic or business justification, have a much tougher path to acceptance because they require people to step outside their comfort zone and readjust their expectations of the workplace. Technology is prone to cause conflict in this area because it is so disruptive, but at the same time, it confers irresistible competitive advantages. Even organizations that have traditionally resisted rapid change feel increasingly compelled to explore new connected and collaborative information tools—out of fear of falling behind, if for no other reason. They then risk being blindsided by the profound effects that these tools can have on processes central to the character of the organizational culture, such as decision making, managerial authority, and transparency of information.

Organizational culture is intimately connected to the generational outlook of the leadership and, to a lesser extent, the broader workforce. Most organizations understand this in a vague way. It is common to hear sentiments expressed like "Oh, blogs won't succeed here because we're an older shop," or "We have a bunch of kids who have a lot to learn, but think the seasoned pros are idiots because they can't use the new software." They recognize the generationally divisive potential of technology but have not found a means of addressing it. They feel forced into a trade-off: either forego the potential benefits of the new technology, or else lose some of the knowledge and productive capability of people and teams to frustration, conflict, and attrition.

Cultures can change through communication, but it is important to know how and what to communicate about. It's not enough to explain the features and functions of a new system or to mandate a time frame for adoption. Because technology now reaches so deeply into life and work, discussions about technology policy are actually discussions about management practices, working conditions, team dynamics, compensation, and career development. Because the largest changes associated with new collaborative information work tools are cultural, not technological, the generational problems created by their implementation have less to do with the relative ease or difficulty of using new software, and more to do with the underlying changes to the patterns of authority implicit in user-created content and widespread collaboration. For example:

Collaborative Decision Making: Collaborative decision making through social networking tools such as reputation systems, collaborative filtering, and information futures markets can help organizations more quickly sort good information from bad and point the way to more effective strategies. These tools also take power away from senior people—often Boomers who spent their entire careers working their way up into roles where they could escape the stultifying group-consensus culture they negotiated since birth and put their cherished ideas into action. Consequently, the benefits of better decision making are understandably lost on those who believe their own decision-making powers are just fine (and hard-earned) already.

"The idea that you're going to open up decision making to a lot of different people is great in theory, but to do that properly, you have to actually believe in it," says Oliver Young, an analyst who covers Web 2.0 technologies for Forrester Research. "You have to have a culture that says if you're going to contribute to this, if you take the time and trouble to participate, it's going to actually make a difference. It isn't going to come down to what one person or one committee thinks. Those sorts of broader cultural changes are what hold a lot of these Web 2.0 deployments back."

The real issue in implementing distributed decision-making tools, then, is not which technology to use, but how to mitigate the loss of power (and perception of value) experienced by managers whose individual judgment has now been superseded by the output of a collaborative community. Until you have *that* conversation within your organization, the questions about technology are merely academic.

Distributed Organizations and Semi-Anonymous Communities: Many participants in online collaborative workgroups and communities of practice have never met in person, even when they work within the same organization. That's part of the point of remote collaboration: getting people together who would not have otherwise met. The problem is, communities of practice, depend on trust and social capital to function. Participants can recognize the benefits of sharing information on an intellectual level, but may be reluctant to do so without having an underlying relationship with their collaborators, especially when the information being shared is sensitive.

Willingness to trust others in anonymous online social environments has nothing to do with technology and everything to do with generational culture. Millennials are as accustomed to social computing environments as their parents are with talking on the telephone. Their trust is, if anything, too high, as evidenced by the ongoing concerns about online sexual predators trolling for partners in chatrooms and MySpace. Older people from the Silent Generation are famously distrustful: most of the OATS students, for example, provide false personal information online as a matter of course and are extremely skeptical when it comes to privacy-related issues. Boomers and GenXers take a balanced view, depending on their experience and sophistication. Organizations hoping to improve the spread of best practices or realize other benefits of remote, interorganizational collaboration, need to address the trust issues alongside the technology issues to get the expected results from their investments.

Knowledge Management: As discussed earlier, preserving the explicit and tacit knowledge of retiring workers is critical to maintaining operational excellence, innovation, and customer relationships. Web 2.0 applications, such as blogs, podcasts, shared workspaces, social networks, RSS feeds, and wikis all provide significantly easier, more flexible, and informal ways for people to contribute knowledge—and more convenient and engaging ways for others to consume it. It's certainly true that younger people often constitute the bulk of users of these systems, but that is not necessarily because there is any technological barrier for older workers. The experience of groups like OATS shows that even the most technologically unsophisticated older people can be acculturated into the tools and practices of collaborative knowledge sharing with remarkably little effort.

Organizations can benefit tremendously from emergent forms of knowledge sharing, which can make the benefits much more tangible and authentic than static, transactional knowledge bases. As these new methods are adopted, they can actually help transform the culture as people internalize the more natural, organic ways to collaborate. Edelman Change and Employee Engagement, a consultancy focused on these issues, highlighted some of the cultural benefits of blogging in the enterprise in a 2006 report:

> The ability of blogs to create a community around issues and events makes them a powerful tool for culture change. By providing a channel for management and employees to share stories, and creating a forum for more open discussion, blogs can help shape a more aware and inclusive organization. "Blogs can help bring humanity back into the workplace," says Michael Wiley, senior vice president with Edelman's me2revolution, who formerly served as Director of Global Communications Technology and New Media at General Motors. "We have become so concerned with communicating numbers and processes that employees have forgotten how to build relationships. *How can companies ask employees to provide superior service and innovative thinking when everything they see and hear flies in the face of that? Blogs help create a culture that supports those behaviors.*"[2] [emphasis added]

The real difficulties with any knowledge management system, even ones based on accessible and emergent technologies, are rooted in the business model and in the way that individual people see their jobs. Senior workers are usually busy doing the things that make them valuable. Silents and older Boomers in particular have a deeply engrained "time is money" attitude and are apt to see activities such as documenting their knowledge and practices as of secondary importance at best. They may also feel pressure to outproduce younger colleagues to demonstrate their continued relevance to the organization. In some industries or job roles, such as professional services or sales, compensation is linked directly to specific activities (e.g., billable hours or closing deals). Spending time doing anything that does not directly contribute to those metrics carries a negative economic incentive to reinforce any social or psychological concerns the worker might have.

The perceived technology problems of older people learning and using new tools like blogs and wikis are a symptom of a larger issue in knowledge retention, which is carving out time, resources, and social space for older workers to document their knowledge and relationships. Even a few minutes a day recording a podcast might be too long for a senior manager if it means losing a sale or missing an important customer call.

Increasingly, professional services organizations such as law firms are creating specific roles to support knowledge creation, learning, and retention. For workers in these roles, knowledge management is not just part of their job—it *is* their job. For example, many leading UK firms have well-developed precedents and know-how systems. These are maintained by full-time professional support lawyers (PSLs), who are senior lawyers (and in some cases partners) and experts in their fields. The functions of PSLs, depending on the firm and the practice group, may include development of precedents, maintenance of know-how databases, filtering and dissemination of current awareness information, and training.[3] These firms have determined that maintaining their knowledge base is worth the profound cultural adjustment of paying a senior professional member of the firm for time outside the hourly billing framework.

Other organizations looking to succeed with knowledge management need to put actual resources, not just good intentions, behind the effort. This means assigning an economic value to knowledge that is as real and concrete to both the worker and the organization revenue from sales and operations. Organizations that are serious about knowledge retention should find ways to start having conversations with both older and younger workers that reflect the priority and value of knowledge, and exploring cultural changes to support those efforts when necessary.

ARE YOU BUILDING BRIDGES, NOT WALLS?

Managing across the digital age gap means harmonizing the strengths of the different generations in the workforce and using technology to unite rather than divide the organization. Left to themselves, workers of different ages will apply their own preconceptions and experiences of technology at work, sometimes leading to conflict and misunderstanding when generational priorities diverge. But when management demonstrates a commitment to respecting both the expectations of younger workers and the concerns of more experienced workers around technology, organizations can effectively combine the tech-savvy of the young with the knowledge and wisdom of the old in ways that make the organization more competitive, more resilient to external change, more efficient, and more open.

Two ways that organizations can build bridges across the digital age gap are *Listening to the Future* (creating formal channels for younger workers to contribute ideas about technology and practices) and *Reciprocal Mentoring* (pairing younger and older workers in formal relationships where older workers provide knowledge and career coaching, and junior employees provide personalized technology training).

Listening to the Future: As we saw in Chapter 8, organizations can tap into the unique experiences and perceptions of digital natives to work through the implications of emerging technology as part of a disciplined visioning process. This can yield surprisingly rich information for long-term strategic business planning, product development, recruitment, and other areas. For employers that don't want to engage in a full-on scenario planning exercise but still want to tap into the insights of younger workers on tactical, near-term issues related to information work and technology, there is an easier way: just ask them.

This could be handled informally in small organizations and workgroups, but there are reasons why a defined process might work better. Young workers are looking to engage and contribute, but are increasingly leery of living up to the stereotype of wanting to run things when they walk in the door. As author and consultant J.T. O'Donnell cautions on "Employee Evolution," a Web site of career advice to younger workers, Millennials can sometimes "hit the work scene, complete a surface assessment, and determine what they think is wrong and should be fixed. They believe in teamwork, and so in a sincere effort to help, they start to make suggestions on how to improve things." Unsurprisingly, this approach often backfires. O'Donnell suggests that "if we want to get older generations (a.k.a. upper management) to actually listen, make changes, incorporate our ideas, and utilize us in a more challenging capacity in the process, we need to prove to them we truly understand and respect their perspective."[4]

Some younger workers may take this advice and sell up their ideas about technology, but they can't gain an understanding and respect for management's perspective in a vacuum. Management, as the senior partner in the relationship, needs to initiate the conversation, provide the context, and show how positive results can emerge from the process. Some steps might include:

- Carve out a safe space to sound out how younger workers think they work best, the tools they prefer, and the ways that they would improve different aspects of the job and the work experience. This allows them to voice their views honestly and openly, without inappropriately confronting managers or seeming presumptuous.

- Bring younger workers and IT professionals together to discuss technology issues in a constructive way. This can help younger workers understand the specific challenges around enterprise IT that may not be obvious from an end-user perspective, and give IT decision makers better insights into the requirements of the more sophisticated users to help in planning decisions.

- Connect workers of different generations specifically to discuss differences in attitudes toward work and technology, and how these differences might impact the potential direction of IT initiatives.

- Challenge younger workers to help solve the cultural and generational issues around technology. Although many younger people are aware of the digital age gap, do not assume that they will automatically consider these factors, or will take a constructive approach to them unless the discussion leader specifically frames them as an aspect of the problem of technology implementation.

- Empower and reward younger workers who use and evangelize new solutions and practices in appropriate ways. Millennials in particular respond well to individual feedback and recognition. Creating incentives for responsible use of technology can be more effective than heavy-handed prohibitions and punitive policies for misuse.

- Recognize the diversity of experience and opinion among younger workers toward technology. Although most younger people have picked up basic skills and familiarity through their experience, there is no uniformity of opinion about the social, political, and cultural implications of the wired world, about which tools and technologies work best, or whether all of this "digital native" stuff is overdone.

- Read the blogs related to employment, generational issues, and technology. A lot of very smart people are giving away up-to-the-minute insights for free on content-rich, well-designed sites, where they may be more candid and direct than they would be in a person-to-person setting (as demonstrated by some of the blog posts quoted elsewhere in this book). The list of resources is too dynamic to commit to print, but be sure to check www.generationblend.com for an updated list of links and contacts.

Creating a formal process for soliciting and incorporating the views of younger workers toward technology does a few important things: (1) it demonstrates that the employer respects the expertise of younger workers; (2) it gives them an early opportunity for legitimate recognition, influence, and value creation; and (3) it provides a constructive alternative to the risky path of neglect.

Reciprocal Mentoring: Mentoring as a knowledge management strategy is nothing new in the business world. When Jack Welch took the helm of General Electric in the 1970s, he instituted a formal mentoring program in which experienced company veterans took new employees under their wings. The experiment paid off. It not only helped GE solve a basic problem of knowledge management and cultural continuity, but it also created bonds of trust between the different generations within the company. Today, more companies have adopted mentoring programs as a strategic approach to addressing the challenges of employee recruitment and retention, succession planning, diversity, and transfer of important tacit knowledge.

Technology and the uneven distribution of skills between older and younger workers opens up a whole new dimension for mentoring, and a whole new set of benefits for organizations that promote it. Consider a few of the things we've discovered in exploring generational issues around work and technology:

- Older people don't like to be singled out for their lack of tech skills, but respond extremely well to personalized, one-on-one training from respectful younger tutors.
- Millennials get along well with their elders, believe in volunteering their time, are hungry for knowledge, and are actively shopping for mentors.
- Senior workers and seasoned experts lack the time and patience to document their knowledge using technology.
- Younger workers need to learn the business, may contribute less immediate revenue than more established workers, and are more confident and familiar with collaborative knowledge tools.
- Organizations are challenged to retain both younger and older workers, and are looking for ways to create loyalty and emotional connections that can help discourage turnover.

Reciprocal mentoring, where young workers who are new to the organization are paired with senior experts for two-way knowledge transfer and coaching, neatly fills a whole panoply of organizational needs and is personally rewarding for the participants as well. The alignment of old and young generations in today's workplace, with young Millennial go-getters eager to learn and crusading elder Boomers eager to teach, is a far more promising environment for reciprocal mentoring than the ill-favored GenX–Veteran/Silent combination prevalent in the early 1990s.

As we saw with the OATS intergenerational program, this approach can be extremely effective once organizations have made the necessary investments in determining the appropriate instructional design, curriculum, materials, and mentor-training methods. Many of the practices employed by OATS and other nonprofit and workforce development groups are transferable to corporate and government environments. Procter & Gamble, Siemens, and GE all have programs that match younger workers with older colleagues to share technology and business knowledge.[5] In 2001, then–GE chairman Jack Welch ordered his 600 top executives to seek out younger colleagues to familiarize them with new e-business practices.[6] The Wharton School of Business at the University of Pennsylvania has also provided some excellent case evidence for reciprocal mentoring practices and outcomes. In 2002, the program matched about 60 executives with graduate students who demonstrated an excellent grasp of technology. The pairs met face-to-face but also exchanged knowledge via e-mail and the phone. "Executives are beginning to realize that knowledge isn't a one-way street. It's in everyone's best interest to share expertise," says Jerry Wind, director of the Wharton Fellows Program.[7] Wind observes that three keys to successful mentoring are:

- Train the mentor to be patient and keep their advice restricted to the relevant topic.
- Ensure the mentor understands the importance of the executive's (mentoree's) critical need for privacy and confidentiality.
- Consider using external mentors for very senior executives if the privacy issue is paramount, and also to manage possible resentment at the junior levels.[8]

One well-established example of reciprocal mentoring in the public sector is the GenYES program that pairs students with teachers in learning partnerships around technology.[9] The goal of the program is to better integrate technology into the classroom, bring teachers up to speed on the latest technology trends that their students are using, and improve student learning by helping younger people develop collaboration, problem-solving, and communication skills. GenYES began as a federal Technology Innovation Challenge Grant in the Olympia school district in Washington State in 1996, and has been adopted by school districts across the country.

Technology mentoring programs can take many forms. They can be straight-up technology training, where younger people tutor older colleagues in nonthreatening, controlled settings, or reciprocal arrangements where the older workers provide coaching and job-specific guidance. They can be strictly within the organization, or reach out to the local community through student internship and apprentice programs. They can be spearheaded by IT, human resources, or within individual departments and operating units. In all cases, the critical factors are mutual respect between the participants and some recognition of the differences in learning styles between older and younger generations.

FINAL THOUGHTS

The intergenerational workforce of the early 21st century is bursting with potential. More than 80 million Millennials are poised to infuse businesses, government, nonprofits, and society at large with their energy, optimism, teamwork, and sense of civic purpose. Millions of GenXers are moving up into management ranks, with their entrepreneurial instincts, practicality, and no-nonsense style well-matched to the realities of a competitive global marketplace. And Boomers stand ready to take their place as elder leaders, guiding organizations with vision, purpose, and commitment well into their older adulthood. Together, this alignment of generations can rebuild damaged institutions, streamline outdated processes, and balance secular achievements with spiritual values. It's a rare historical moment, and we'd do well to make the most of it.

New technology gives us a powerful magnifier for these different strengths. It connects us to vast resources of information, systems, and human expertise. It makes opaque processes transparent. It brings collective knowledge resources to bear on specific problems and illuminates patterns within chaotic jumbles of data. It can help ease the tensions between work and life, and collapse the boundaries of physical distance.

Technology is also a centrifuge that, through its relentless speed, can separate us out into isolated strata, divided from one another according to our degrees of comfort and competence with the new tools of work. Age and generational outlook are natural friction points that technological innovation can exacerbate. Technology is not neutral or unbiased with respect to age. It is created for the young, by the young, and sold into the enterprise through a very narrow channel of decision makers who do not always consider the impact of new tools on the people whose talents constitute the organization's differentiated value.

Organizations can minimize the friction and amplify the potential of their investments in both people and technology by noting the ways that new connected information tools transform and disrupt traditional practices and relationships, then taking steps to address those issues in ways that account for generational differences. That's not a one-time effort, but the beginning of a longer process.

The generational picture is certain to evolve. The characteristics of each cohort are observable, and their interactions subject to informed conjecture, but nothing is set in stone. The same is exponentially true of technology. The next innovation could change everything and render all of the concerns expressed here about conflicting priorities and tolerance for complexity quaint and irrelevant. In 25 years at most, the pre- and post-digital divide in the workforce will be a thing of the past—doubtless replaced by some other form of generational strife.

In the meantime, we have a lot of information available about the challenges and opportunities formed by the collision of demographics, globalization, and connected information technology that characterizes the first decade of the 21st century, where the workforce is made up of generations on either side of a transformational divide. Not all of these observations apply to every organization and certainly not to every individual. More evidence is needed from organizations that have tackled these issues head-on, so managers can choose from a range of good practices appropriate to their needs. Fortunately, one defining characteristic of the connected world is that the dialogue is always moving forward. Every contribution to the discourse changes the conditions at least a little bit by moving people to a greater state of awareness about themselves and their actions. The growing volume of work being done on this subject—in academia, through commercial research, on blogs, and in books like this one—is bound to cause some change even as it observes the changes that are already taking place. Knowledge will grow, people will learn, better ideas will replace ones grown old and stale, and practices will adapt to new realities.

Hopefully this book has given you some new information to consider when approaching these issues in the here and now. I invite everyone to keep the conversation going and share your experiences and insights at www.generationblend.com.

ENDNOTES

1. Pollard, Dave. "Communication Tools: Make them Simple and Ubiquitous or They Won't Be Used." *How to Save the World Blog*, posted May 29, 2007. http://blogs.salon.com/0002007/2007/05/29.html

2. "New Frontiers in Employee Communications, 2006." Edelman Change and Employee Engagement/PeopleMetrics, 2006. http://www.edelman.com/image/insights/content/NewFrontiers2006_Finalpaper.pdf

3. Kay, Stewart. "Features—Benchmarking Knowledge Management in U.S. and UK Law Firms." *LLXR*, August 15, 2002. http://www.llrx.com/features/benchmarkingkm.htm

4. O'Donnell, J. T. "Why 'Managing Up' Is Worth the Trouble." Employee Evolution (Web site), July 5, 2007. www.employeeevolution.com/archives/2007/07/04/getting-older-generations-to-listen-%e2%80%93-why-%e2%80%98managing-up%e2%80%99-is-worth-the-trouble/

5. Dyctwald, Erickson, and Morrison, *Workforce Crisis*, p. 82.

6. Starcevich, Matt M. "What Is Unique about Reverse Mentoring, Survey Results." Center for Coaching and Mentoring, 2001. www.coachingandmentoring.com/reversementoringresults.htm

7. Greengard, Samuel. "Moving Forward with Reverse Mentoring—Sharing the Knowledge." *Workforce*, March 2002. http://findarticles.com/p/articles/mi_m0FXS/is_3_81/ai_84148619

8. Quoted in "Mentoring Connections Newsletter." *The Growth Connection*, February 2005. www.growconnect.com.au/archives/Feb05.html

9. "GenYES—A Proven Model for School-wide Technology Integration ." Generation Yes, 2007. www.genyes.org

Acknowledgments

This book would not have been possible without the support of many people. First and foremost, this work and this author owe a huge debt of gratitude to Dan Rasmus, whose insight, encouragement, and friendship have contributed immeasurably to my personal and professional development, and without whom there would literally be no project for me to have undertaken. Thanks also to Sam Hickman and Amy Cole at Microsoft for bringing the book series to life and having confidence in me to get this project completed on time.

Credit for the thoroughness and scope of the references goes to my resourceful and patient researcher, Rebecca Alexander. The blame for any errors or misrepresentations of the information rests solely with the author.

My colleagues at MediaPlant—Guy Roadruck, Miguel Mitchell, and Chris Munson—went above and beyond to help with the production of charts and figures, as well as the gathering and transcription of interviews. They also designed and executed the website at www.generationblend .com and produced the audiovisual materials for my speeches and presentations in support of this book.

Tim Burgard and his team at John Wiley & Sons could not have made this process any easier for a perplexed first-time author facing a daunting deadline. Seriously, Tim, this was supposed to be harder. Many thanks are also due to Jan Shanahan at Wildsky Industries for keeping the project moving and taking the time to offer support and advice.

When I was asked to submit a proposal for this series, my first call was to my dear friend and OATS Executive Director, Tom Kamber. I was thrilled he agreed to be part of this project. Tom, along with Renée Martinez, Dee Derr Daugherty, and the staff and board of OATS, were unbelievably generous with their time and insights. Thanks also to OATS program participants Beverly Daffner, Ida Harris, Thai Jason, Lester Johnson, Marcia Kinsey, Cheryl Mahnis, Vivian Notturno, Jennifer Pellegrino, and Nia Reyes for sharing their wonderful experiences and giving this work a human voice.

Prashant Ratna Kansakar, Joey Manke, Jake Donovan, and Vasisht Srinivasan agreed to share their fresh insights on the world of work from the perspective of people just starting out in the workforce. Discussions with various GenX entrepreneurs and managers, including Chad Romanesko, Kylie Hanson, Joseph Gleason, Tony Martinelli, and Melinda Neely, were more helpful than they might have imagined. Thanks also to members of the Microsoft Board of the Future, who allowed their remarks to be quoted for this work.

During the course of writing this book, James Barrett, Russ Eckel, Ryan Healy, J. T. O'Donnell, Dave Pollard, Edward Tenner, Penelope Trunk, and Oliver Young of Forrester Research generously shared their expertise on various facets of this topic in conversation, or allowed me to quote from their blogs.

Paul Andrews, Russ Eckel, Neil Howe, Richard Salkowitz, Susan Salkowitz, Joe Santos, Erik Smith, Daniel Sosnoski, William Strauss, John Underkoffler, and Mark White were kind enough to review the draft manuscript and offer helpful suggestions and encouragement.

LoRayne Apo-Joynt and David Partikian provided additional research. Min Yee helped me track down information on the Generation Yes project in the Seattle schools.

Finally, all my thanks and love to my biggest fan and most perceptive critic, my wife Eunice Verstegen, who put up with me being even worse than usual during the writing of this book.

Index